AGRICULTURE ISSUES AND POLICIES

U.S. FARM BUSINESSES AND THE ROLE OF DEBT

USE PATTERNS AND KEY TRENDS

AGRICULTURE ISSUES AND POLICIES

Additional books in this series can be found on Nova's website under the Series tab.

Additional e-books in this series can be found on Nova's website under the e-book tab.

AGRICULTURE ISSUES AND POLICIES

U.S. FARM BUSINESSES AND THE ROLE OF DEBT

USE PATTERNS AND KEY TRENDS

LAURA C. HUGHES
EDITOR

nova publishers
New York

Library of Congress Cataloging-in-Publication Data

ISBN: 978-1-63483-734-7

Published by Nova Science Publishers, Inc. † New York

CONTENTS

PREFACE

Farm businesses' debt-use decisions can affect their growth and survival, as well as the economic vitality of farm-dependent rural communities. Thus policymakers, agricultural lenders, and other farm-sector participants closely follow trends in farm debt. This book is a primer on the use of debt by U.S. farm businesses for policymakers, researchers, and others interested in the financial well-being of U.S. agriculture. It presents data on basic debt-use patterns by farm businesses (in 2011, over 900,000 farms operated as farm businesses based on their size, organizational structure, or the occupation of their principal operator) and explores key trends over 20 years. U.S. farm debt use varies widely by farm size, specialization, operator age, and other farm characteristics.

In: U.S. Farm Businesses and the Role of Debt ISBN: 978-1-63483-734-7
Editor: Laura C. Hughes

Chapter 1

DEBT USE BY U.S FARM BUSINESSES, 1992-2011*

Jennifer Ifft, Amirdara Novini and Kevin Patrick

ABSTRACT

This report is a primer on the use of debt by U.S. farm businesses for policymakers, researchers, and others interested in the financial well-being of U.S. agriculture. It presents data on basic debt-use patterns by farm businesses (in 2011, over 900,000 farms operated as farm businesses based on their size, organizational structure, or the occupation of their principal operator) and explores key trends over 20 years. U.S. farm debt use varies widely by farm size, specialization, operator age, and other farm characteristics. Large-scale farm businesses, farm businesses with younger operators, and dairy and poultry farm businesses all have higher levels of debt use. Both average debt-to-asset ratios and the share of farm businesses with high debt-to-asset ratios have declined over time.

Keywords: Farms, debt, debt-to-asset ratios, commodities, agricultural resource management survey

---

* This is an edited, reformatted and augmented version of Economic Information Bulletin Number 122, issued by the U.S. Department of Agriculture, Economic Research Service, April 2014.

WHAT IS THE ISSUE?

Farm businesses' debt-use decisions can affect their growth and survival, as well as the economic vitality of farm-dependent rural communities. Thus policymakers, agricultural lenders, and other farm-sector participants closely follow trends in farm debt. During the early 1980s, farm income plummeted and interest rates rose rapidly, which contributed to numerous farm bankruptcies and rural bank failures. Today, the farm sector overall is in a strong financial position after several years of generally rising income. However, the potential for lower income and higher interest rates in the future has raised concerns about current trends in the use of debt by farm businesses. This study analyzes how farm businesses used debt from 1992 through 2011, with a focus on the considerable heterogeneity among farm businesses in their debt obligations.

WHAT DID THE STUDY FIND?

While total debt held by farm businesses increased 39 percent from 1992 to 2011 (after adjusting for inflation), the average farm business debt-to-asset ratio was 0.13 in 1992, rose to 0.15 in 1997, and declined to 0.09 in 2011. Further, the share of highly leveraged farm businesses (those with a debt-to-asset ratio greater than 0.40) has declined since 1992, as has the share of the value of production contributed by highly leveraged farms.

The broad types of debt used by farm businesses were relatively stable from 1992 to 2011—total debt was comprised of about 60 percent real estate debt, 20 percent non-real-estate debt, and 20 percent short-term debt throughout the entire period.

Although stable overall, U.S. farm debt use varied widely by farm size, specialization, operator age, and other farm characteristics.

Key factors that influenced debt use include:

- *Farm business size and organization.* Large-scale family farms (those with annual gross cash farm income of $1 million or more) hold the largest share of farm business debt (about 35 percent). The share of debt held by these farms has increased since 1992, while the share held by small-scale family farms with a farming occupation (farms whose principal operator has farming as his or her primary occupation and annual gross cash income less than $350,000) has declined.

- *Commodity specialization*. Farm businesses specializing in dairy and poultry production have the highest average debt-to-asset ratios (0.19 and 0.18 in 2011, respectively) while field crop, specialty crop, and beef farm businesses have the lowest debt-to-asset ratios (0.10, 0.10, and 0.06 in 2011, respectively).
- *Region*. Debt-use levels vary by region, but these differences are not as substantial as between the other categories considered in this study. In 2011, farm businesses in the Northern Crescent had the largest average debt-to-asset ratio (0.12), and farm businesses in the Basin and Range had the smallest (0.07). These patterns largely reflect regional differences in the types of farm commodities produced.
- *Operator's age*. Farm business debt-to-asset ratios decrease as operator age increases. While most age groups experienced an overall decline in debt-to-asset ratios over 1992-2011, the youngest group (age 34 or younger) did not experience a substantial decline in financial leverage. Farmland purchases and ownership may play an important role in these trends.

U.S. farm business debt share by type of debt, 1992 versus 2011

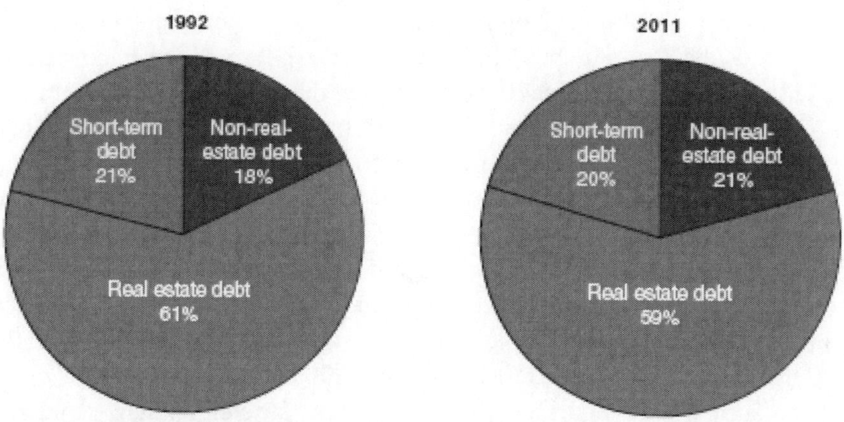

Source: USDA, Economic Research Service and National Agricultural Statistics Service; 1992 Farm Costs and Returns Survey and 2011 Agricultural Resource Management Survey.

How Was the Study Conducted?

This study was conducted using data from the Farm Costs and Returns Survey (1992-95) and the Agricultural Resource Management Survey (1996-2011), which were both conducted jointly by the U.S. Department of Agriculture's Economic Research Service (ERS) and National Agricultural Statistics Service. The study considered only farm businesses—family farms with annual gross cash farm income of $350,000 or more, smaller family farms whose principal operator reports farming as his or her major occupation, and nonfamily farms—which held about 79 percent of all farm debt and made up 42 percent of all U.S. farms in 2011. Farm businesses were separated into four subcategories (small family farms that had farming as their major occupation, midsize family farms, large-scale family farms, and nonfamily farms) based on the ERS farm typology. Gross cash farm income was adjusted for inflation when classifying farm businesses, and the key variables considered were debt uses, total debt, and debt-to-asset ratios.

Introduction

The use of debt by farm operators can signal both financial strength and the willingness or need to take on financial risk. If the return on debt-financed assets exceeds the cost of debt, debt use will increase farm income and wealth. However, increasing use of debt also increases the financial risk that a farm faces (including the risk of bankruptcy) if farm revenues are lower than expected. Farm operators have different risk preferences, or inclinations to take on a certain level of risk, and a farm's debt level is a business decision made between the operator and the financial institution or other source of borrowed capital. However, decisions regarding use of debt at the farm level can have implications for the entire farm sector and for the rural businesses that serve this sector. For example, a wave of farm bankruptcies in the early 1980s, caused by declining farm income and a rapid increase in interest rates, led many agricultural lenders to belatedly adopt stricter lending standards (including basing loan decisions on farm income instead of collateral). During this period, many farm businesses were forced to liquidate assets as working capital dried up, while many rural banks failed and the economic sectors that supported agriculture declined (Barnett, 2000).

Given its broader economic implications, policymakers and bank regulators are concerned with farm debt use. Today's near-record levels of farm income have led to comparisons between the past decade and the decade leading up to the farm crisis in the 1980s, and concerns about similarities in debt use. While average farm income and debt use increased during both periods, there are also many differences. The structure and organization of the farm sector, agricultural lending practices, and the overall macroeconomic environment have all changed substantially over the past 30 years. Hence, concerns about debt use are best considered in the context of current farm financial conditions.

The U.S. farm sector has had several years of relatively high and increasing farm income since 2000. Since 2011, inflation-adjusted farm-sector income has been at near-record levels (USDA/ERS, 2013). These high-income levels, combined with increasing farmland values, have allowed farmers to increase overall debt while reducing their financial leverage (as measured by their level of debt relative to the value of their assets). Total debt held by farm businesses increased 39 percent from 1992 to 2011 in inflation-adjusted terms. Likewise, inflation-adjusted farmland values nearly doubled from 1992 to 2011, due to increasing farm income, decreasing interest rates, and various other factors (Nickerson et al., 2012). Increasing production and machinery expenses also put upward pressure on debt use.

Historically low interest rates over the past 5 years have lowered the cost of debt financing and made it a more attractive option for farmers. Lenders may also rate more farmers as qualified borrowers due to low interest rates. Many forecasts predict a decline in farm income and an increase in interest rates (Schnitkey, 2013; Westcott and Trostle, 2013), and either prediction could make high levels of farm debt riskier for both lenders and borrowers, although agricultural lending practices are typically conservative relative to other sectors of the economy. For example, most farmland purchases require a down payment that is a larger share of total value than for housing purchases. However, risks are not uniform across the U.S. farm sector. U.S. farms' use of debt is as diverse as the farm sector itself, with debt use varying widely by farm size, specialization, operator age, and other farm characteristics.

This study considers basic debt-use patterns from 1992 to 2011 by farm businesses, which are defined as small family farms whose operators designate farming as their main occupation, family farms with gross cash farm income (GCFI) over $350,000 (midsize and large scale), and nonfamily farms. Farm businesses have consistently held around 80 percent of total farm debt and made up less than half of all U.S. farms over the 20 years studied (see

Table 1). The average farm business debt-toasset ratio was 0.13 in 1992, rose to 0.15 in 1997, and declined to 0.09 in 2011.

This report is a primer on the use of debt by farm businesses for policymakers, researchers, and others interested in the financial health of the U.S. farm sector. While this report will not provide statistical analysis of farm business debt use, it will provide suggestions for future research in this area.

Table 1. Farm business characteristics, 1992 versus 2011

	1992	2011
Number of farm businesses*	954,400	908,900
Share of all farms	46%	42%
Share of farm debt	77%	79%
Percent with no debt**	44%	57%
Debt-to-asset ratio	0.13	0.09

Source: USDA, Economic Research Service and National Agricultural Statistics Service; 1992 Farm Costs and Returns Survey and 2011 Agricultural Resource Management Survey.

Note: *Rounded to the nearest 100, **no debt is defined as debt-to-asset ratio less than 0.01.

FARM BUSINESS DEFINITION

This report identifies two major types of farms—family farms and nonfamily farms—as farm businesses (based on the latest USDA, Economic Research Service farm typology (Hoppe and MacDonald, 2013)):

- Family farms are defined as farms with majority ownership by the principal operator's household and relatives in other households. Family farms are further subdivided into the following categories for this report:
    - Small farms are those with real gross cash farm income (GCFI) less than $350,000. Small farms whose operators claim farming as their primary occupation are classified as farming-occupation farms with either low sales or moderate sales (which were combined for this study). Small farms whose principal operator reports being retired from agriculture (retirement farms) or their primary occupation as something other than farming (off-farm

occupation farms) are excluded from this study because they generally have less debt and rely on off-farm income.

- Midsize family farms are those with GCFI between $350,000 and $999,999, and
- Large-scale family farms have GCFI of $1 million or more. These farms are further divided into two categories, large and very large, based on GCFI (which were combined for this study).

- Nonfamily farms are all other farms, including partnerships of unrelated operators where none of the partners holds a majority of the farm or a farm owned by absentee heirs of the previous owner where the operator is a hired manager. As of 2011, 78 percent of nonfamily farms had GCFI less than $350,000.

Table 2. Farm characteristics by classification, 2011

	Farm businesses	Retired/off-farm occupation	All farms
Number of farms*	908,900	1,263,900	2,172,800
Share of all farms	42%	58%	100%
Share of farm debt	79%	21%	100%
Percent with no debt**	57%	74%	67%
Debt-to-asset ratio	0.09	0.06	0.08
Avg. debt per farm***	$153,200	$29,200	$81,100

Source: USDA, Economic Research Service and National Agricultural Statistics Service; 2011 Agricultural Resource Management Survey.

Note: *Rounded to the nearest 100, **no debt is defined as debt-to-asset ratio less than 0.01, ***average debt for all farms in each category.

Farm business classification

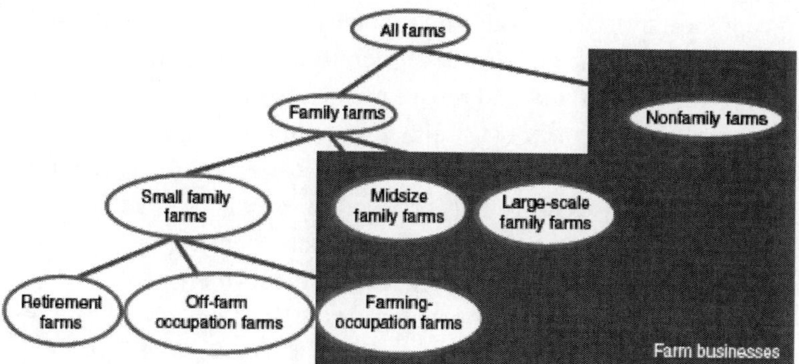

Source: USDA, Economic Research Service.

Data Sources

This study uses data from the 1996-2011 Agricultural Resource Management Survey (ARMS) and the 1992-1995 Farm Costs and Returns Survey (FCRS), a predecessor to the ARMS, which were both conducted jointly by the U.S. Department of Agriculture's Economic Research Service (ERS) and National Agricultural Statistics Service. Given the long timeframe of the study, it was necessary to adjust the selection criteria for farm businesses for inflation. For example, a farm that made $350,000 in 1992 would be much larger in terms of quantity of production than a farm that made $350,000 in 2011. When determining farm typology classifications in each year, we used the Producer Price Index (PPI) deflator to adjust GCFI to real 2011 dollars, following the recommendations of White and Hoppe (2012). After adjusting for inflation, GCFI of $350,000 in 2011 is equivalent to GCFI of $194,200 in 1992. The 1992 FCRS did not identify retired farmers, so respondents over the age of 70 were assumed to be retired that year.

FARM DEBT USES

The major types of debt used by farm businesses did not change substantially over the 20 years studied (Figure 1). The type of debt held (whether short-term debt, real estate debt, or longer term, non-real-estate debt) provides information on how debt is being used, as well as loan conditions and maturity. Short-term debt is classified as any debt—including production loans—lasting less than 1 year, while non-real-estate debt includes loans with a maturity greater than 1 year but not secured with a lien on real estate. (Debt for each category and throughout this report is measured as the balance owed on December 31—therefore, short-term debt does not include any short-term (or operating) loans taken out and repaid within the year.)

The majority of farm debt is either used to purchase real estate or is secured with a lien on farm real estate (while real estate loans could be used for machinery purchases or other production expenses, most are used to purchase real estate or refinance real estate debt). With some small fluctuations, the share of debt held by farm businesses between 1992 and 2011 has roughly been 60 percent real estate debt, 20 percent long-term non-real-estate debt, and 20 percent short-term debt.

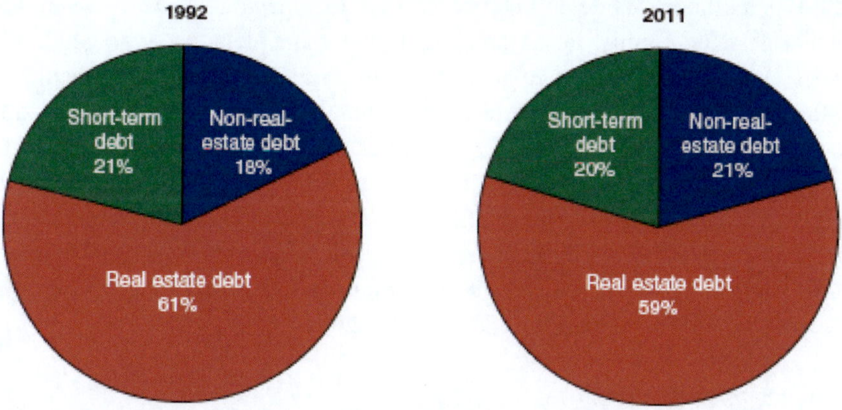

Source: USDA, Economic Research Service and National Agricultural Statistics Service; 1992 Farm Costs and Returns Survey and 2011 Agricultural Resource Management Survey.

Figure 1. U.S. farm business debt share by type of debt, 1992 versus 2011.

Debt by Type of Farm Business

Farm size and organization are major factors influencing farm debt use. While total farm business debt increased from $100 billion in 1992 to $139 billion in 2011 (in constant 2011 dollars using the chain-type deflator (White and Hoppe, 2012)), the contribution of different farm business types to total farm business debt also changed (Figure 2). The share of farm business debt held by large-scale family farms increased from 16 percent in 1992 to 35 percent in 2011 (table 3). The share of debt held by small family farms with a farming occupation has declined from 46 percent of all farm business debt to 27 percent over the same period. The value of production created by farm businesses has shifted similarly. In 1992, small family farms contributed the greatest share of the value of production of farm businesses (35 percent), and large-scale family farms contributed only 24 percent. In 2011, large-scale family farms contributed 37 percent and small family farms 20 percent of the value of production. The share of debt held by midsize family farms and nonfamily farms, and the value of production created by these farm types, stayed relatively constant over the 20 years studied.

The average debt held per farm is another key indicator of debt-use trends. For large-scale family farms, average debt increased by about 70 percent from $684,400 in 1992 to $1,165,500 in 2011 (in constant 2011 dollars using the chain-type deflator (White and Hoppe, 2012)). Compared to 1992, there are now more large-scale family farms and they have more debt on average. In this respect, debt-use trends are related to broad structural changes happening in the farm sector. The average debt held by midsize family farms increased by about 16 percent from 1992 ($263,800) to 2011 ($305,900) after adjusting for inflation, while the average debt held by small family farms decreased by about 9 percent (from $61,300 to $55,600). Together, these trends indicate that most of the growth in farm business debt from 1992 to 2011 is attributable to large-scale family farms. Debt held by nonfamily farms increased by about 58 percent from $153,600 to $244,100 (on average).

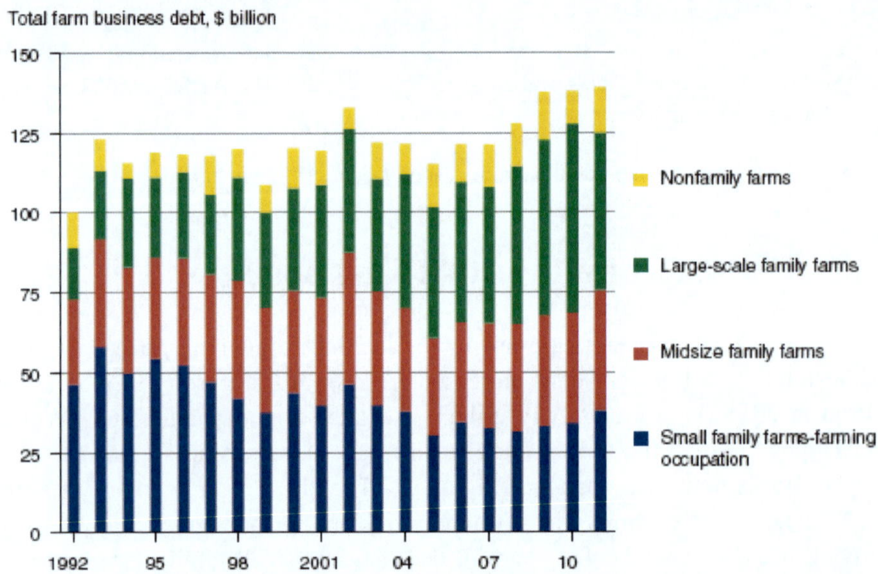

Source: USDA, Economic Research Service and National Agricultural Statistics Service; 1992-1995 Farm Costs and Returns Survey and 1996-2011 Agricultural Resource Management Survey.

Figure 2. Total U.S. farm business debt, by type of farm business.

Table 3. Share of farm business debt and value of production by type of farm business

Debt			Value of production	
1992	2011	Farm type	1992	2011
11%	10%	Nonfamily farms	18%	16%
16%	35%	Large-scale family farms (GCFI ≥$1 million)	24%	37%

Debt			Value of production	
1992	2011	Farm type	1992	2011
26%	27%	Midsize family farms (GCFI $350,000-999,999)	23%	27%
46%	27%	Small family farms-farming occupation (GCFI<$350,000)	35%	20%

Note: Percentages are based on debt and value of production for farm businesses only. GCFI refers to gross cash farm income.

Source: USDA, Economic Research Service and National Agricultural Statistics Service; 1992 Farm Costs and Returns Survey and 2011 Agricultural Resource Management Survey.

DEBT USE BY FARM BUSINESS COMMODITY SPECIALIZATION

Different farm commodity specializations have different financing requirements, so their debt use varies significantly. Debt-to-asset ratios are a key measure of a farm's leverage, or the degree to which farm assets are financed by debt. Higher debt-to-asset ratios indicate a higher reliance on borrowed funds and generally coincide with a higher likelihood of loan default. Although several measures are necessary to comprehensively evaluate the financial health of a farm operation, the debt-to-asset ratio is a widely used measure of financial risk. Debt-to-asset ratios tend to increase as farm size increases, and they also vary by farm specialization. While the debt- to-asset ratio that implies vulnerability to insolvency varies based on individual farm business characteristics, a commonly used threshold is a debt-toasset ratio greater than 0.40 (for example, in Harris et al., 2009).

Dairy and poultry farm businesses are generally more leveraged than farms specializing in the production of other commodities (Figure 3). These specializations generally face higher capital costs, which contribute to increased debt use. Dairy farms were more leveraged in 2011 than in 1992, on average, because the dairy sector underwent significant structural change during this period and average farm size increased substantially (MacDonald et al., 2007). Capital expenditures necessary to increase farm size may have contributed to the higher average debt-to-asset ratio for large-scale family dairy farm businesses.

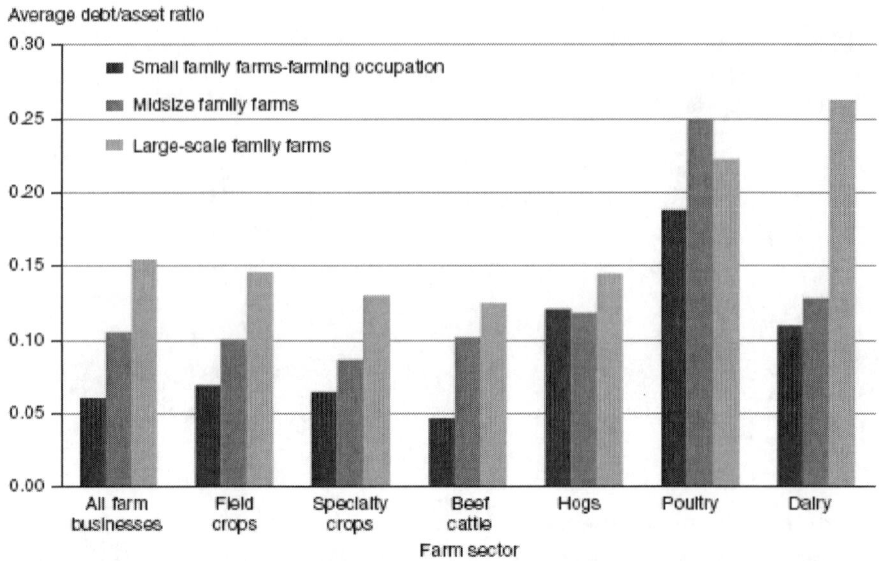

Source: USDA, Economic Research Service and National Agricultural Statistics Service; 2011 Agricultural Resource Management Survey.

Note: Farm business specializations are determined by the commodity or group of commodities constituting the majority of the farm's total value of production. Nonfamily farms are excluded due to concerns about statistical reliability.

Figure 3. Average debt/asset ratio of U.S. farm businesses by specialization and size, 2011.

Large-scale family poultry farms have slightly lower leverage than midsize family poultry farms; however, this difference is not statistically significant. Further, the majority of poultry farm businesses fall into either the small or midsize family farm business categories.

For example, around 70 percent of poultry farms with production contracts had only one to four poultry houses in 2006. Poultry houses are also likely to be debt financed (MacDonald, 2008), leading to small and midsize family poultry farm businesses having substantially higher leverage than similar farm business types with other specializations.

Field crop, beef, and hog farms, on the other hand, had relatively large reductions in leverage between 1992 and 2011. Crop farm businesses, in particular, have likely benefited the most from increasing farmland values, and this may be reflected in their relatively low debt-to-asset ratios. Beef and hog farm businesses had levels of leverage similar to field and specialty crop farm businesses in 2011, with the exception of small family farms that specialize in hog production. Large-scale family farms that specialize in hog production have substantially more cropland acres on average than similar poultry farm businesses (almost five times as many cropland acres operated in 2011) and lower financing costs than similar dairy farm businesses, which may explain why their debt-toasset ratio is relatively lower. Beef cattle farm businesses have lower average capital investments than other livestock farms, which might contribute to their relatively low debt-to-asset ratio.

Farm Business Debt Use by Region

Average farm business debt-to-asset ratios vary by region (Figure 4), although the differences are not as striking as by specialization or by farm size. In 2011, farm businesses in the Northern Crescent had the largest average debt-to-asset ratio (0.12), and farm businesses in the Basin and Range had the smallest (0.07). The average debt-to-asset ratio has fallen for all regions since regional data collection started in 1996, with the largest reductions occurring in the Mississippi Portal and the Basin and Range regions.

Several factors can affect these regional differences, including farm size, specialization, lending institutions, and risk preferences/culture. Dairy farm businesses are more prominent in the Northern Crescent, while farm businesses are more likely to operate on a larger scale in the Northern Great Plains, contributing to higher average debt-to-asset ratios in these two regions. Farm businesses in the Southern Seaboard tend to be smaller than in most other regions, while farm businesses in the Basin and Range are more likely to specialize in beef or "other livestock" (mainly sheep and horse production) than businesses in other regions, contributing to lower regional debt-to-asset ratios.

Farm Business Debt by Operator Age

The average age of farm business operators rose over the 20 years studied (table 4). In 1992, 30 percent of all principal farm business operators (the operator primarily responsible for day-to-day management decisions) were younger than 45 years old, and 48 percent were older than 55. In 2011, 13 percent of principal farm business operators were younger than 45, and 68 percent were older than 55. The share of farm businesses with principal operators from age 45 to 54 was similar in 1992 and 2011.

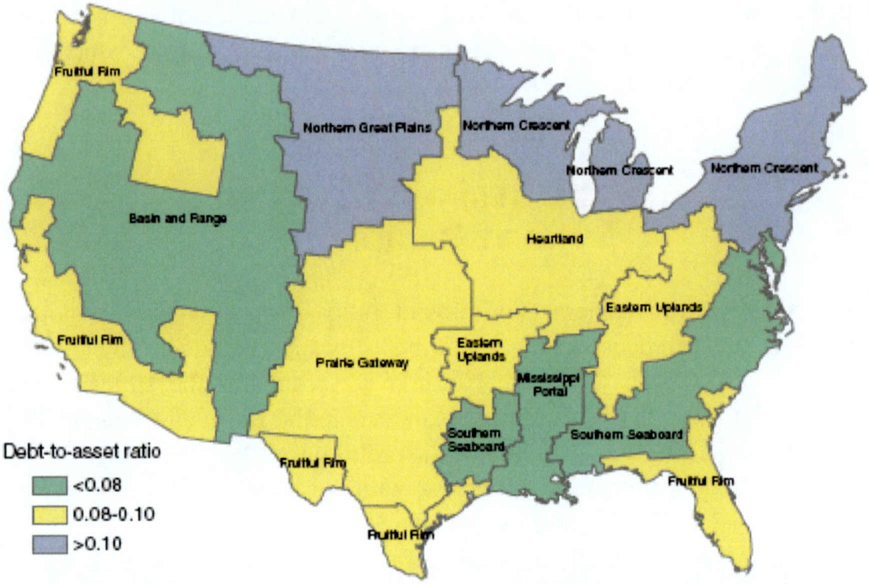

Source: USDA, Economic Research Service and National Agricultural Statistics Service; 2011 Agricultural Resource Management Survey.

Note: These are ERS U.S. Farm Resource Regions. For more information, see http://webarchives.cdlib.org/wayback.public/UERS_ag_1/20111128195215/http:/ www.ers.usda.gov/Briefing/ARMS/resourceregions/resourceregions.htm

Figure 4. Average U.S. farm business debt-to-asset ratios by region, 2011.

It is best to consider a relative measure of debt, such as the debt-to-asset ratio, to understand the changes in farm debt use by operator age over time because the sheer increase in the number of operators 55 and older makes comparing absolute debt levels between the age groups over time less informative. As expected, farm business debt-to-asset ratios have largely been decreasing over the past two decades, and debt-to-asset ratios also tend to decline as farm business operators age (Figure 5). Young operators use debt to expand their farm operation, adopt new technologies, and improve competitiveness and profitability. Older operators are more likely to have paid off farm debts and are less likely to take on new debt as they approach retirement. Therefore, operator age is a key factor in farm business debt-use trends.

Younger operators (34 or younger) had similar leverage in 2011 as in 1992. However, operators in the 35-44 and 45-54 age categories experienced an overall reduction in leverage, although there is considerable year-to-year variation in average debt-to-asset ratios for these age groups. Upticks in leverage for these age groups in the last 5 years may have been due to loans taken out to purchase increasingly expensive farmland during this period. Production expenses also increased during this time and may be another contributing factor. Older operators (age 55-64 and 65 up) also experienced an overall decline in leverage since 1992. Additionally, while all age categories experienced significant fluctuations in leverage that largely correspond to farm income levels in a particular year (such as 2002), operators age 55 and older experienced significantly less variation in their average leverage in the later half of the study period. This may be due to these operators owning more farmland than other age categories and being less likely to take out new loans. Further, because older operators are less likely to expand their operations, higher farm income during the later half of the period may have allowed older operators to use less debt for production expenses. The role of real estate debt and farmland ownership in debt use by different operator age groups is an important topic for future research, as is the impact of an aging farm operator population on debt-use trends.

Table 4. Proportion of farm business principal operators by age group, 1992 versus 2011

	1992	2011
Less than 45 years old	30%	13%
45 to 54 years old	22%	19%
55 years old and older	48%	68%

Source: USDA, Economic Research Service and National Agricultural Statistics Service; 1992 Farm Costs and Returns Survey and 2011 Agricultural Resource Management Survey.

HIGHLY LEVERAGED FARM BUSINESSES OVER TIME

The share of farm businesses with high debt-to-asset ratios has declined over time. In addition to average debt-to-asset ratios, a more robust picture of farm debt use emerges by considering changes in the number of highly leveraged farms (Figure 6). Specifically, we consider two categories of farm businesses based on the leverage categories used by Harris et al. (2009):

- *Category I:* Farm businesses with debt-to-asset ratios between 0.41 and 0.70, and
- *Category II:* Farm businesses with debt-to-asset ratios greater than 0.70.

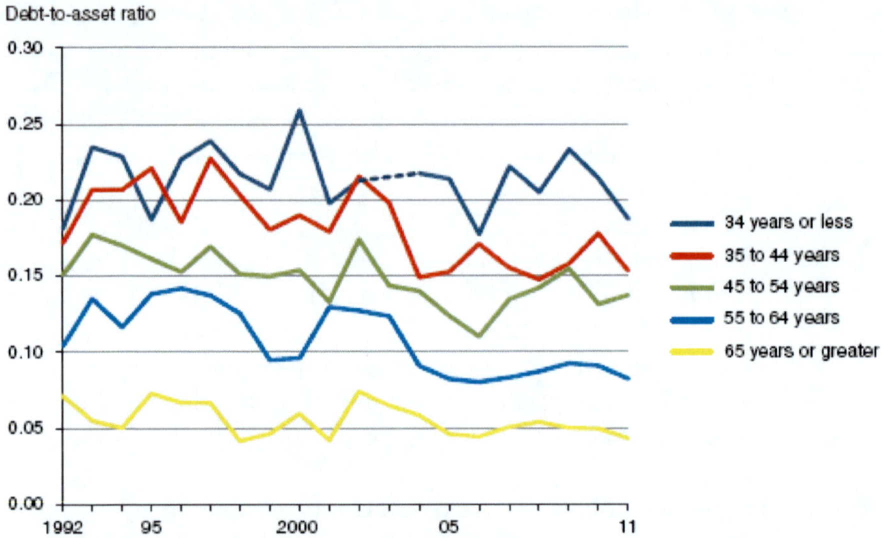

Note: The dashed line indicates that the debt-to-asset ratio for operators 34 years or younger was imputed for 2004 due to concerns about statistical reliability.

Source: USDA, Economic Research Service and National Agricultural Statistics Service; 1992-1995 Farm Costs and Returns Survey and 1996-2011 Agricultural Resource Management Survey.

Figure 5. Farm business debt-to-asset ratios by principal operator age, 1992-2011.

Over time, the shares of crop and livestock farm businesses that were highly leveraged declined. Between 1993 and 2011, the share of farm businesses with debt-to-asset ratios exceeding 0.4 was halved (to less than 6 percent). In 1993, almost 10 percent of crop farms were in *Category I,* and more than 4 percent were in *Category II.* By 2011, the share of farm businesses falling into these two high-leverage categories had declined to 4 percent and 1 percent, respectively. Among livestock farm businesses, over 8 percent were in *Category I* and 2 percent were in *Category II* in 1993, declining to less than 4 percent and 1 percent, respectively, by 2011.

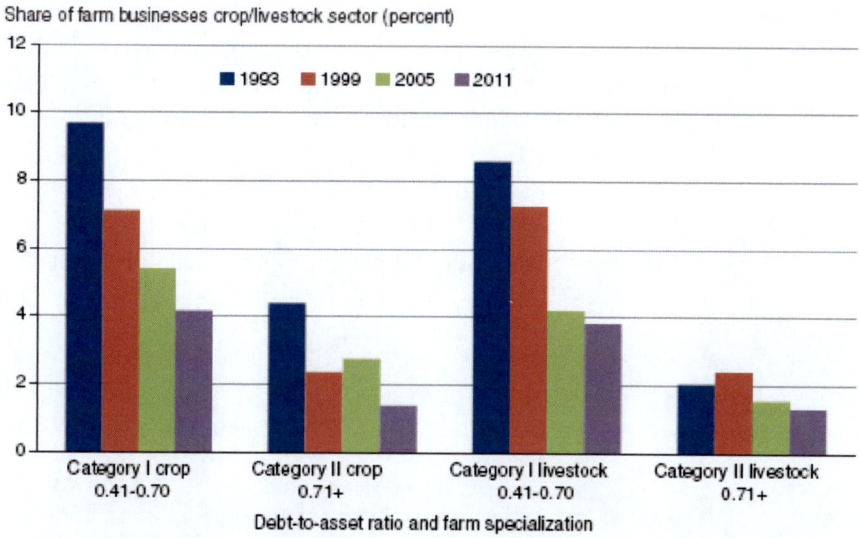

Source: USDA, Economic Research Service and National Agricultural Statistics Service; 1993 Farm Costs and Returns Survey and 1999, 2005, and 2011 Agricultural Resource Management Surveys.

Note: These two farm business specializations, crop and livestock, are determined by the specialization which constitutes the majority of each farm's total value of production. *Category I* farm businesses have debt-to-asset ratios between 0.41 and 0.70, and *Category II* farm businesses have debt-to-asset ratios greater than 0.70.

Figure 6. Shares of crop and livestock farm businesses with high leverage, 1993-2011.

CONTRIBUTIONS TO VALUE OF PRODUCTION BY HIGHLY LEVERAGED FARM BUSINESSES

While the number of highly leveraged farm businesses has decreased over time, the contribution of these farms to the total value of production is also important, as it indicates the vulnerability of production to changes in debt levels. The declines in the share of the value of production attributed to highly leveraged farm businesses have largely been proportionate to the declines in the number of farm businesses with high leverage. Farm businesses in *Category I* (debt-to-asset ratio between 0.41 and 0.70) had an average value of production that was consistently twice the average for all farm businesses. In

Category I, 8 percent of farm businesses contributed 16 percent of farm businesses' total value of production in 1992 (Figure 7). By 2011, 4 percent of *Category I* farm businesses contributed 9 percent of the total value of production.

The share of farm businesses in *Category II* (debt-to-asset ratio above 0.70) has declined slightly since 1992, and this group's share of the value of production has also declined slightly (although the overall downward trend is not as clear as with *Category I*). The value of production for farm businesses in *Category II* was between two and three times as large as the share of farm businesses in *Category II*: in 2011, 1.3 percent of farms were in *Category II*, and these farm businesses contributed 3.9 percent of the value of production. These shares may have spiked in 2002 and 2009 due to declines in farm income.

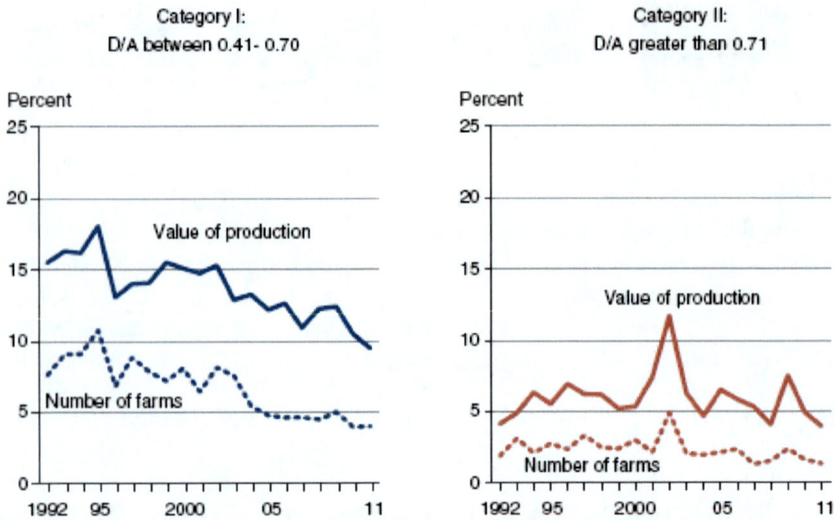

Source: USDA, Economic Research Service and National Agricultural Statistics Service; 1992-1995 Farm Costs and Returns Survey and 1996-2011 Agricultural Resource Management Survey.

Note: D/A stands for debt-to-asset ratio, with higher ratios corresponding to higher financial leverage and risk.

Figure 7. Share of farm businesses with high leverage and share of value of production, 1992-2011.

Conclusion

This report highlights many of the factors influencing farm business debt use, such as farm size, commodity specialization, region, and operator age. Many of the differences in the use of debt by farm businesses are related to structural changes in the farm sector over the 20 years studied. Average leverage has declined across most of the farm categories considered in this study, and the share of farms that are highly leveraged, as well as their share of total farm business value of production, has declined over time. While older operators and crop farms are more likely to have benefited from increasing farmland values, livestock farms were also less leveraged in 2011, on average, than they were in 1992. Younger operators, large-scale family farms, and dairy and poultry farm businesses currently have the riskiest financial positions as measured by their average debt-to-asset ratios. However, if farm income declines or interest rates increase, most farm businesses appear to be better positioned to withstand the resulting loan payment shocks than they were in the early 1990s.

While this report provides a descriptive analysis of past farm business debt use, more research is needed to predict how current debt use would be affected by changes in financial conditions. Multiple changes could affect farm financial well-being, including a rise in interest rates, decline in farm real estate values, changes in farm and energy policy, and changes in international trade. The debt-carrying capacity of farm businesses that are more highly leveraged, such as those specializing in dairy and poultry production, may be more vulnerable to changes in these variables. Other areas of interest for future research include use of variable-rate loans, the impact of changes in interest rates, and the use of debt substitutes (such as production contracts or leasing farmland). A comprehensive financial ratio analysis for different farm types (which includes various measures of liquidity, profitability, and operating efficiency in addition to leverage) would also provide useful information on the financial health of farm businesses.

References

Barnett, B. J. "The US Farm Financial Crisis of the 1980s," *Agricultural History*, (74:2), Spring, 2000.

Harris, J., J. Johnson, J. Dillard, R. Williams, and R. Dubman. The Debt Finance Landscape for U.S. Farming and Farm Businesses, AIS-87, U.S. Department of Agriculture, Economic Research Service, November 2009. Available at: http://www.ers.usda.gov/media/153616/ais87.pdf (accessed June 2013).

Hoppe, R., and J. MacDonald. Updating the ERS Farm Typology, EIB-110, U.S. Department of Agriculture, Economic Research Service, April 2013. Available at: http://www.ers.usda.gov/publications/eib-economic-information- bulletin/eib110.aspx (accessed July 2013).

MacDonald, J. The Economic Organization of U.S. Broiler Production, EIB-38, U.S. Department of Agriculture, Economic Research Service, June 2008. Available at: http://www.ers.usda.gov/publications/eib-economic-information-bulletin/eib38.aspx (accessed December 2013).

MacDonald, J. M., E. O'Donoghue, W. McBride, R. Nehring, C. Sandretto, & R. Mosheim. Profits, Costs, and the Changing Structure of Dairy Farming, ERR-47, U.S. Department of Agriculture, Economic Research Service, September 2007. Available at: http://www.ers.usda.gov/publications/ err-economic-research-report/err47.aspx (accessed December 2013).

Nickerson, C., M. Morehart, T. Kuethe, J. Beckman, J. Ifft, and R. Williams. Trends in US Farmland Values and Ownership, EIB-92, U.S. Department of Agriculture, Economic Research Service, February 2012. Available at: http://www.ers.usda.gov/publications/eib-economic-information-bulletin/eib92.aspx (accessed December 2013).

Schnitkey, G. "Management Implications of Non-Decreasing Interest Rates," Farmdoc Daily, November 26, 2013. Available at: http://farmdocdaily.illinois.edu/2013/11/management-implications-non-decreasing-interest-rates.html (accessed December 2013).

The White House. "Economic Report of the President," March 2013. Available at: http://www.whitehouse.gov/sites/default/files/docs/erp2013/full_2013_economic_report_of_the_president.pdf (accessed July 2013).

U.S. Department of Agriculture, Economic Research Service. 2013 Farm Sector Income Forecast. Available at: http://ers.usda.gov/topics/farm-economy/farm-sector-income-finances/2013-farmsector-income-forecast.aspx (accessed December 2013).

Westcott, P., and R. Trostle. USDA Agricultural Projections to 2022, OCE-131, U.S. Department of Agriculture, Economic Research Service, February 2013.Available at: http://www.ers.usda.gov/ publications/oce-usda-agricultural-projections/oce131.aspx (accessed December 2013).

White, T. K., and R. Hoppe. Changing Farm Structure and the Distribution of Farm Payments and Federal Crop Insurance, EIB-91, U.S. Department of Agriculture, Economic Research Service, February 2012. Available at: http://www.ers.usda.gov/media/261681/eib91_1_.pdf (accessed August 2013).

In: U.S. Farm Businesses and the Role of Debt ISBN: 978-1-63483-734-7
Editor: Laura C. Hughes

Chapter 2

THE DEBT FINANCE LANDSCAPE FOR U.S. FARMING AND FARM BUSINESSES*

J. Michael Harris, James Johnson, John Dillard, Robert Williams and Robert Dubman

ABSTRACT

Income and wealth for farm businesses have changed noticeably this decade. Debt levels have been rising, asset levels have outpaced debt despite a recent fall in land prices, and equity has more than doubled for farm businesses. However, recent declines in farm income and falling land prices have raised concerns about the financial position of U.S. farms. Total farm sector debt reached a record $240 billion in 2008, a $26-billion increase over 2007. Debt is expected to decline to $234 billion in 2009. The distribution of debt among farm operators has also been changing. In 1986, nearly 60 percent of farms used debt financing. By 2007, the number had dropped to 31 percent. In essence, farm debt has become more concentrated in fewer, larger farm businesses. Lenders and farm operators indicate that real estate accounts for the largest use of farm debt. Debt repayment capacity utilization (DRCU) of farm operators has dropped since the 1980s. DRCU dropped from 27 percent in 2000 to 22 percent in 2007. Larger farms are more likely to use more of their debt capacity.

---

* Citation Note: This is an edited, reformatted and augmented version of a report, AIS-87, issued by the U.S. Department of Agriculture, Economic Research Service, November 2009.

EXECUTIVE SUMMARY

Recent disruptions to commodity and financial markets have raised concerns about the financial position of U.S. farms. The rise in commodity prices in 2007 and early 2008 ended in late 2008. Since then, falling commodity prices have dimmed farm income prospects for 2009, and tightened cash flows have stalled the impressive growth in farm asset values experienced over the last 20 years. Despite the sector's long-term financial strength, these developments have created concerns that farmers may be unable to meet debt service obligations and pay household expenses if financial conditions worsen.

To put these developments into perspective, this report first looks at the farm debt situation. U.S. farm sector debt was an estimated $214 billion in 2007, a nominal record high for the third consecutive year. Preliminary forecasts are for farm sector debt to be an estimated $240 billion in 2008 and $234 billion in 2009.

Although debt is at record levels, this fact alone is not a reason for great concern. Until 2009, the growth in agricultural assets and equity had far outpaced growth in debt. Net farm income, although variable, has trended upward over the last two decades. Farm income growth, along with competition for farmland for nonfarm uses, has driven up the value of agricultural land, which accounts for 87 percent of farm assets. With higher farm returns and a larger collateral base, the farm sector is in a better position to borrow and repay farm debt than it was 20 years ago. The sector's debt-to-asset ratio fell from 21 percent in 1986 to less than 10 percent in 2007. Put another way, lenders had a claim on more than one-fifth of farm assets in 1986; by 2007, they had a claim on only one-tenth of farm assets.

In addition to sectorwide trends, this report also examines financial trends among farm businesses. Not all stakeholders in U.S. agriculture are considered farm businesses—landlords and other stakeholders hold a significant amount of the agricultural sector's assets and debt. To focus more closely on farm operators, the Agricultural Resource Management Survey (ARMS) is used to examine their financial health and behavior through 2007 (the most recent farm-level data available).

Farm businesses reported an estimated $140 billion of debt in 2007, which accounted for nearly two-thirds of the U.S. farm sector's total debt. Much like farm sector debt, the amount of debt held by farm operators has increased substantially since 1990. Although farm business debt has been more variable, it remains near its nominal record high, set in 2006.

The distribution of farm business debt has also been changing. The share of farm operators that use debt to finance their operation is declining. In 1986, nearly 60 percent of farm operators used debt to finance their operation. By 2007, this figure had dropped to 31 percent. Since loan volume has increased over time, this indicates that debt usage has become more concentrated in fewer farm businesses.

The distribution of debt among farm businesses is not uniform. Larger farms, with their greater asset bases and higher revenues, are much more likely to use debt than smaller farms. Larger farms are more often operated on a full-time basis and require more land, machinery, equipment, and input supplies than smaller farms. Additionally, farmers who operate poultry, hog, and dairy farms have adopted more intensive production practices and require larger facilities than the typical farm, and are much more likely to use debt to finance their operations.

The relationship between debt use and organizational complexity also emerges from our analysis. The majority of U.S. farms are small, part-time, or retirement operations, with a sole owner-operator. However, the majority of U.S. agricultural output is generated by large operations with multiple owners and operators. The share of large, complex business organizations using debt to finance their operations was much larger than that of smaller, less complex operations.

Debt is also not evenly distributed among farm operators. The share of farmers using debt is inversely related to both operator age and years on the farm. Furthermore, operators who farm as their primary source of income are more likely to use debt, as are farmers that rent some or all of the land they operate.

Lenders and farm operators both indicate that real estate is the single largest use of farm debt. This is not surprising since real estate accounts for such a large proportion of the farm asset base. Other significant uses of farm debt include equipment and machinery loans and short-term operating loans. Lenders reported that 65 percent of funds loaned to farm businesses was intended for real estate purposes, while 20 percent was for intermediate-term loans and 15 percent for short-term operating loans.

Commercial banks and the Farm Credit System accounted for over three-quarters of the farm sector's loan volume (45 and 36 percent, respectively) in 2007. Their share of farm debt has been increasing as the share of loans extended by the Farm Service Agency and individuals (land contracts) has decreased. Nearly three of every five farm operators who used debt used only one lender and one loan to finance their business.

Unused debt repayment capacity for farm businesses has increased since the 1980s. Debt repayment capacity utilization (DRCU), a measure that takes into account debt obligations in relation to maximum debt repayment capabilities, is a good indicator of financial stress. The DRCU for farm operators as a whole is relatively sound, having dropped from 27 percent in 2000 to 22 percent in 2007.

As with farm debt, the level of DRCU is not uniform among farm businesses. Larger farms are more likely to use more of their debt repayment capacity. Operations with less than $100,000 in sales have a DRCU of 14 percent, while farms with over $1 million in sales have utilization figures that are twice as high at 28 percent. Capital-intensive farms—such as dairy, poultry, and hog operations—have a DRCU that is significantly higher than the national mean. In the case of dairy and poultry operations, the level of DRCU has increased since 2007.

INTRODUCTION

U.S. farm businesses have benefited from robust income and wealth gains this decade. Though debt levels have risen steadily, asset levels have risen faster, leading to a doubling of farm business equity since 2000. Despite healthy financial metrics, recent disruptions in domestic and global markets have raised concern about the financial position of U.S. farms.

The rise in farm commodity prices, particularly in 2007 and early 2008, ended in late 2008 as consumer spending stalled and credit became more difficult to obtain. The combination of lower prices for farm products, continued high prices for farm inputs, and tightened cash flows have created concerns that farmers may be unable to meet debt service obligations and pay household expenses.

Farm debt has been a topic of recurring and often intense interest on the part of lenders, regulators, and policymakers. To put concerns over farm debt into perspective, we examine both changes in debt levels and debt costs, and also changes in farmers' income and asset values. Changes in income affect repayment capabilities and thus affect credit safety and soundness. Meanwhile, changes in asset values determine the leverage position or solvency of farms.

While a series of record income years enhanced farmers' debt service capability and growth in farm asset values strengthened the collateral supporting farm loans, a recent downturn in both income prospects and real estate values may have spillover effects on farm lending (Morehart, 2009;

Ellinger, 2009). As credit conditions tighten throughout the U.S. economy, is the financial structure of farm businesses still sound enough to attract and service the debt capital the sector needs?

To address this question, this report:

1) Looks at how much debt is used to finance U.S. agriculture and how debt use has changed over the last 20 years;
2) Determines how much business-related debt is used by farm operators;
3) Examines the characteristics of farms and farm operators owing business-related debt;
4) Examines the purposes for which farmers obtain debt financing;
5) Determines the types of loans used by farmers and their sources; and
6) Assesses the debt repayment capacity of U.S. farms.

Measuring Debt at the Sector and Farm Business Level

To assess debt use and the distribution of debt, USDA's Economic Research Service (ERS) examines two measures of debt—sector debt and farm business debt. The following explanation contrasts the two measures and explains the procedure for estimating both series.

Debt represents claims on a firm's assets by creditors who make capital available for use in the business. ERS incorporates this definition into its estimate of the amount of debt used in U.S. agriculture by preparing balance sheet financial statements that summarize farm assets and debts for two distinct purposes. One provides estimates for farming as a sector of the U.S. economy. At this level, the balance sheet includes the "value of all physical plants which the Census of Agriculture... calls farms" (Irwin, 1968). The other view examines farms as individual business units. The determination of who holds debt and is responsible for its repayment and who owns assets used in farming is a major difference between estimates prepared for the agricultural sector of the national economy and for farms as business operations. A second major difference between the sector and farm-level estimates is the source of data used to prepare balance sheet financial statements.

At the sector level, agriculture is viewed as "one large farm. " Estimates of sectorwide business debt reflect only debt incurred by those involved in onfarm agricultural production. Debt held by firms or individuals that perform input supply, processing, distributing, or marketing functions for farms is excluded from debt and balance sheet measures. [1] Sectorwide estimates of the amount of debt used in farming are the sum of the amount of debt for farm business purposes that is either reported by lenders or derived from national survey and Census of Agriculture data (see Appendix for a discussion of debt at the farm sector and farm business levels). Survey and census-based data are also used to develop estimates of the amount of debt provided by individuals and other non-bank lending institutions.

Sector-level estimates of farm debt report aggregate lender data that do not identify who owes the debt. The borrower could be a farm business owner; an owner of assets--such as farmland, machinery, or livestock--leased by a farmer; or a nonfarm individual or firm involved in farm production, such as the production of livestock or crops under contract. Contractors, who tend to be large processing firms that are not considered part of production agriculture, may, for example, use debt financing to acquire young animals, buy feed, or purchase trucks for use in transporting animals or feed. Likewise, landowners may finance land purchases or, in their capacity as landlords, buy inputs for use in farm production. Lenders report these types of debt as farm debt based on their connection to farm production and assets.

At the farm level, ownership and business boundaries are taken into account. Farm business debt is reported only for the farm as an individual business operation. Debt owed by others, such as landlords or contractors, who have a stake in the business operation, is not included in estimates of farm business debt. Likewise, assets and income that belong to these stakeholders are not considered in developing the farm balance sheet, income statement, or other financial statements, or in preparing performance indicators for the farm.

For purposes of this report, sector-level estimates of debt are used to develop a comparative analysis of changes in total debt use over time for farming as a sector of the U.S. economy. Sector-level debt estimates are then used in conjunction with estimates of assets, equity, and income generated within the sector to provide a farm economy-wide view of debt use, capital structure, and debt service capability.

Since sector-level estimates are developed using aggregate data from a variety of sources, they cannot be used to address issues related to the distribution of debt among farms. Distributional issues are addressed through use of farm-level estimates obtained from USDA's Agricultural Resource Management Survey (ARMS). The ARMS is an annual survey of farms, conducted jointly by the National Agricultural Statistics Service (NASS) and ERS. ARMS provides data needed to construct financial statements and performance indicators for farms and farm households.[2] The characteristics of farms and farm operators that use debt in their business operations and the attributes of their farm loans are also identified. Since similar survey instruments have been used by ERS since the 1980s, farm-level data can also be used to conduct a comparative analysis of changes in the level and concentration of debt among farms over time.

TRENDS IN AGRICULTURAL DEBT

- The nominal value of debt held by farm businesses and other agricultural stakeholders has increased steadily since the mid-1980s. However, debt peaked in 2008 and is projected to decrease slightly in 2009, while still remaining above its 2007 level.
- The amount and share of farming assets owned by farm operators has increased as the share of claims held by lenders has decreased. Lenders' share of farm assets fell from 22 percent in the 1980s to 14 percent in 2008.
- Farm income growth and the decrease in leverage have reduced the sector's debt repayment capacity utilization (DRCU) over the last 20 years. However, DRCU is projected to increase in 2009.

In this section, we look at changes in debt and associated measures since the 1980s. Estimates of debt are used in conjunction with estimates of assets, equity, and income generated within the sector to provide a farm economy-wide view of changes in debt use, capital structure, and debt service capability.

Sector Debt Levels on the Rise

Since undergoing a multi-year retrenchment in the 1980s, with debt for farm purposes bottoming out at $131 billion in 1989, nominal farm debt has exhibited a near steady annual increase over the past two decades. In only 3 of the past 20 years did farm debt not expand, and in one of those years (1992), debt was down less than 0.5 percent. As a result, year-end debt levels reached new nominal records in 2005 and in each year thereafter through 2008 (Figure 1).

Based on data assembled from lending institutions or acquired from farm surveys, U.S. farm sector debt reached an estimated $240 billion by year-end 2008 and is forecast at $234 billion for 2009.[3] While not a record, 2009's forecast year-end debt would still be the second largest nominal amount for the sector. Annual changes in farm sector debt, while highly variable, have still trended higher in recent years (Figure 2).

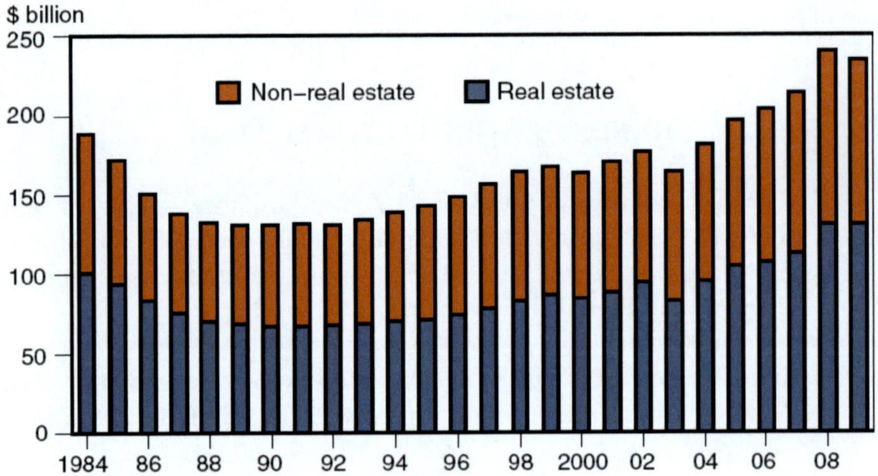

Source: USDA, Economic Research Service.

Figure 1. U.S. farm sector debt, 1984-2009f.

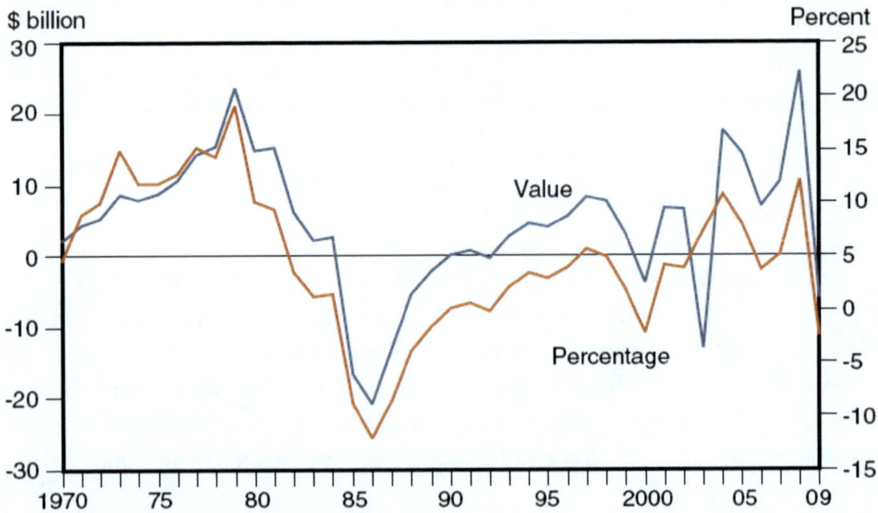

Source: USDA, Economic Research Service.

Figure 2. Changes in U.S. farm sector debt, 1970-2009f.

Debt classified by lenders as being for real estate purposes accounted for 53 percent of total farm sector debt in 2007 and 52. 6 percent in 2008. While this is down slightly from the 54-55 percent of sectorwide debt registered in the mid-1980s, real estate debt has remained roughly 50-53 percent of farm sector debt over the past two decades. The relatively stable share of real estate and non-real estate debt likely reflects farmers' ongoing need to use debt financing for a fairly stable mix of inputs—from acquiring increasingly expensive machinery, equipment, and inputs to the purchase of farmland, buildings, and other structures.

Changes in land prices have been key to changes in the demand for real estate debt (Lins, 1972). Meanwhile, changes in non-real estate debt are positively associated with expenditures for production inputs and capital items, such as machinery and equipment (Williams, 1987). Additional factors that affect the demand for non-real estate debt in U.S. agriculture include the amount of working capital available to farm stakeholders and non-real estate interest rates.

Total Debt Use Also on the Rise for Farm Businesses

The agricultural sector includes farm businesses, institutional farms (e. g., reservations, prison farms, etc.), and nonoperator landlords, along with other stakeholders such as individuals or businesses engaged in contractual arrangements with farm operators. ARMS data allow us to examine the portion of the farm sector accounted for by farm operators. USDA began tracking debt use among farm operators at the individual farm level in the mid-1980s. [4] Farm debt volume reported by farm operators tracks changes in sectorwide debt use. Like sectorwide estimates of debt, the volume of debt reported by farm businesses bottomed out in 1989 (at about $80 billion). In the 20 years since, farm-level business debt has trended upward and stood at $140 billion at the end of 2007, the last year for which farm survey data are available (Figure 3). [5] Comparisons of sectorwide and farm business-level debt indicate that debt has expanded slightly faster for farm businesses than for other stakeholders or for non-business uses of farm debt by farm households (see box, "Farm Operators Only a Subset of Farm Sector Borrowers"). At the farm level, the annual increase in debt averaged 4. 2 percent from 1989 through 2007; the comparable change for sectorwide debt was 3. 5 percent.

Debt Stays Low Relative to Stakeholders' Asset and Equity Values

An increase in the level of debt used in farming may be perceived as drawing down the farm sector's credit reserve. And depending on the prevailing view of prospective farm earnings and underlying collateral values, growth in debt outstanding may be regarded as financially troublesome. But debt, by itself, is only part of the story. Debt levels need to be examined relative to the value of equity contributed by farmers and other stakeholders, and relative to the amount of income available to meet debt service and other funding requirements.

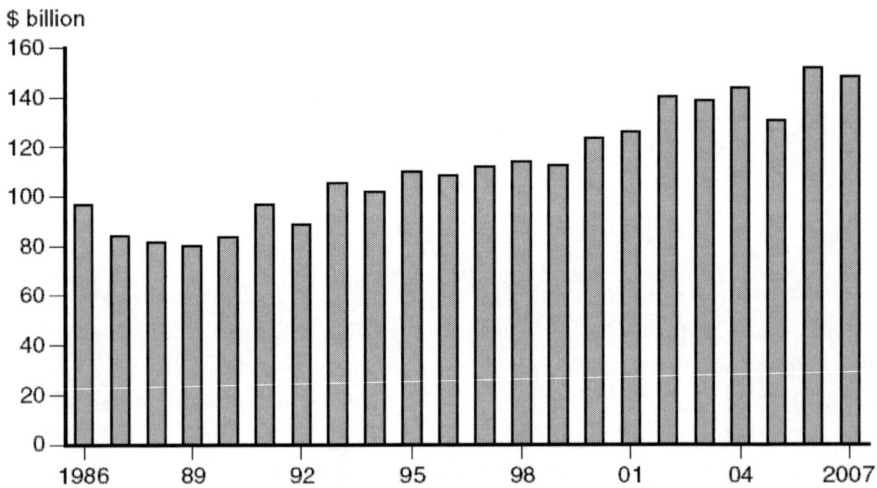

Source: USDA's Agricultural Resource Management Survey, sponsored jointly by NASS and ERS.

Figure 3. Farm-level debt (1986-2007).

Farm Operators Only a Subset of Farm Sector Borrowers

Responses to USDA surveys indicate that farm owner-operators owed 64 percent of total farm sector debt in 1986 and 65 percent in 2007. Between 1986 and 2007, farmers' share of the farm sector's total business debt varied between 65 and 80 percent.

The remainder of farm sector debt is owed by farmers who use farm assets to secure debt for major household purchases or to fund other activities; by non-operator landlords, persons, or businesses that engage in farm production contracts; and by other stakeholders that participate in farming. An example of sectorwide farm-related debt that would be excluded from farm-level business debt is farm operator debt used to finance a limited liability company to hold land, machinery, or equipment leased to a farming operation. Another example is debt used to finance the purchase of cattle placed in a feed- lot by an individual or firm that had no other connection to farming. A land ownership survey in Iowa confirms the participation of stakeholders other than farmers in farm real estate markets (Duffy and Smith, 2008).

Asset values are important in the broader view of farm debt. The relationship between debt and its underlying collateral base indicates both the degree of leverage in U.S. agriculture and the share of total assets provided by creditors, farm owners, or other stakeholders engaged in agriculture.

Asset values for the U.S. farm sector have steadily increased in the two-plus decades following the farm crisis of the 1980s, recording annual increases each year from 1986-87 through 2007 (figure 4). After reaching a low of $722 billion in 1986, sectorwide asset values increased nearly three-fold to $2. 1 trillion in 2007. In 2008, however, the nominal value of farm sector assets decreased for the first time since 1986, and is projected to decrease again in 2009.

Land, the single largest asset in farming, has underpinned the increase in the sector's asset values. The per-acre value of land has increased nearly every year over the last two decades. Real estate, which accounted for 75 percent of total farm sector assets in 1986, stood at 85 percent of farm sector assets in 2007. Lower farm sector asset values in 2008 and 2009 are largely due to reduced farm real estate values.

Farm-sector equity (the difference between asset values and debt) has also risen significantly, reaching a nominal record high nearly every year between 1996 and 2007 (Figure 5). Quite simply, increases in sectorwide asset values outpaced the increases in debt during these years (Figure 6). Not only did equity rise to new nominal highs, but the share of total assets accounted for by owner equity rose from 79 percent in 1986 to 90 percent in 2007. Even with 2008's reduction in asset values and the projected decline in 2009, equity will still account for about 88 percent of the total value of assets in U.S.

agriculture. In 1980, equity accounted for 83 percent of the sector's total asset value.

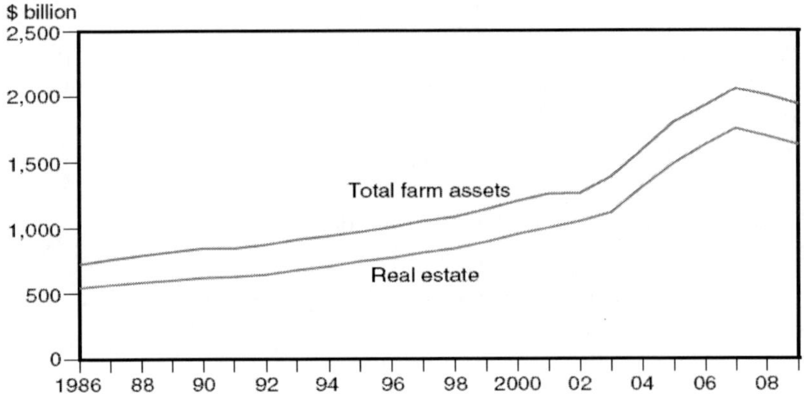

Source: USDA, Economic Research Service.

Figure 4. Farm sector assets, 1986-2009f.

The increase in the value of assets and equity has altered the farm sector's capital structure. Debt relative to the total value of assets used in agriculture has fallen over the past 10 years, particularly between 2003 and 2007 when sectorwide asset values rose 10 percent per year in nominal terms. Thus, creditors' claims on assets have fallen from more than one dollar out of five during the 1980s, to about one dollar out of eight in 2009 (Figure 7). As a result, the risk exposure of both farm asset owners and farm lenders has been reduced.

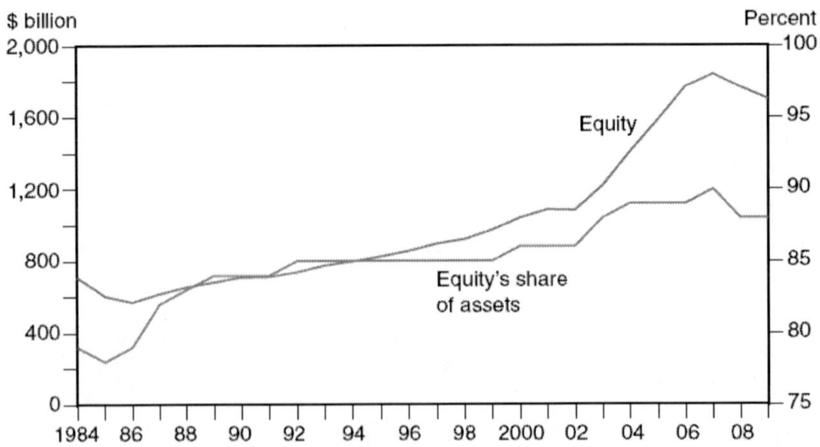

Source: USDA, Economic Research Service.

Figure 5. Farm sector equity, 1984-2009f.

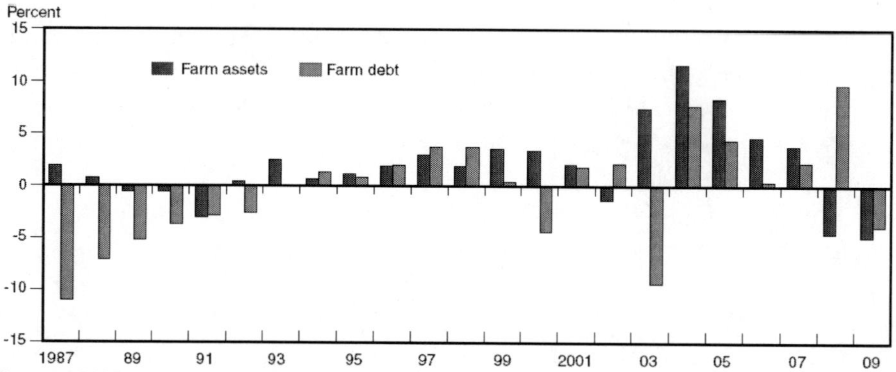

Source: USDA,Economic Research Service.

Figure 6. Comparing farm sector asset growth to debt growth, 1987-2009f.

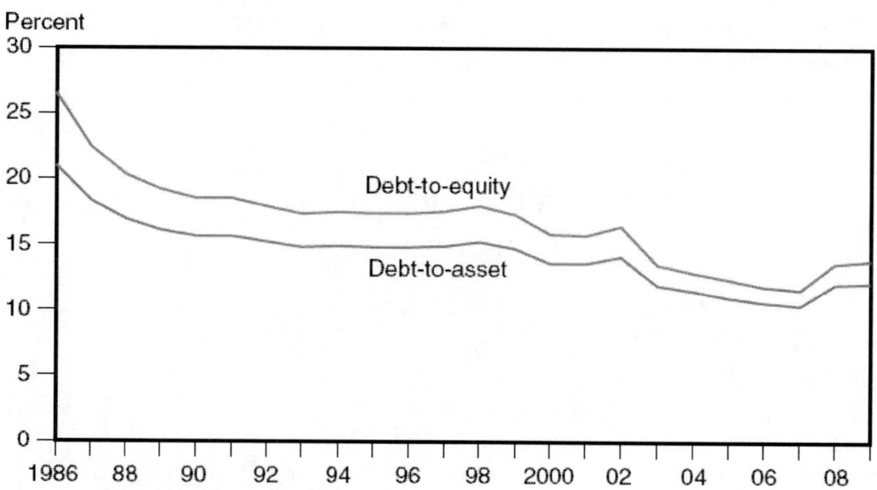

Source: USDA, Economic Research Service.

Figure 7. U.S. farm sector debt-to-asset and debt-to-equity ratio, 1986-2009f.

Debt Relative to Assets and Equity at the Farm Level

For farm business operators, asset values increased in nominal value from \$445 billion in 1986 to \$1. 9 trillion in 2007--nearly 300 percent (Figure 8).[6]

The increases recorded for farm-level asset values greatly surpass the expansion in debt use. In the more than two decades of ongoing annual measurement of farm-level debt and asset values, year-over-year asset values have dropped only three times (Figure 9). In most years, not only did the rate of increase in asset values exceed debt use, but the absolute increase in asset values far surpassed the change in debt. As a result, farm operators posted a 365-percent increase in equity from 1986 to 2007.

Debt in relation to both equity and assets has dropped significantly to less than half the level it was when farm-level balance sheets were first estimated. The farm-level debt-to-asset ratio was estimated to be 0. 22 in 1986, but stood at 0. 08 in 2007, a drop of nearly two-thirds. The drop in debt volume in relation to the amount of assets owned means that farm operators are providing a much larger share of the capital used in farming, and that farms have become significantly less leveraged (Figure 10).

Changes in equity in relation to debt also indicate that the capital structure of farm operators has been much improved during the past two decades. Debt stood at 27. 8 percent of the equity held in farm businesses in 1986; this ratio fell to 8. 6 percent by 2007 (Figure 10). This means that farm operators have a greater ownership stake in their businesses. Consequently, across all farmers, lenders have a smaller stake in farm assets and both farmers and lenders have less financial risk exposure from farm business debt than was the case when farm businesses emerged from the 1980s crisis years and throughout the 1990s.

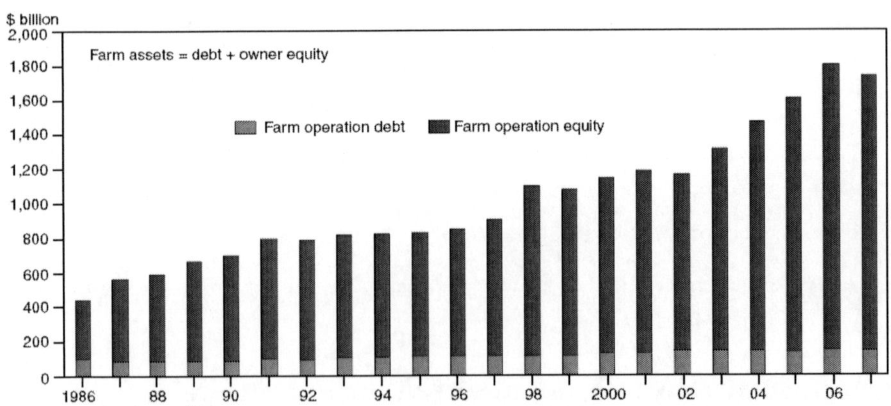

Source: USDA's Agricultural Resource Management Survey, sponsored jointly by NASS and ERS.

Figure 8. Farm business capital structure, 1986-2007.

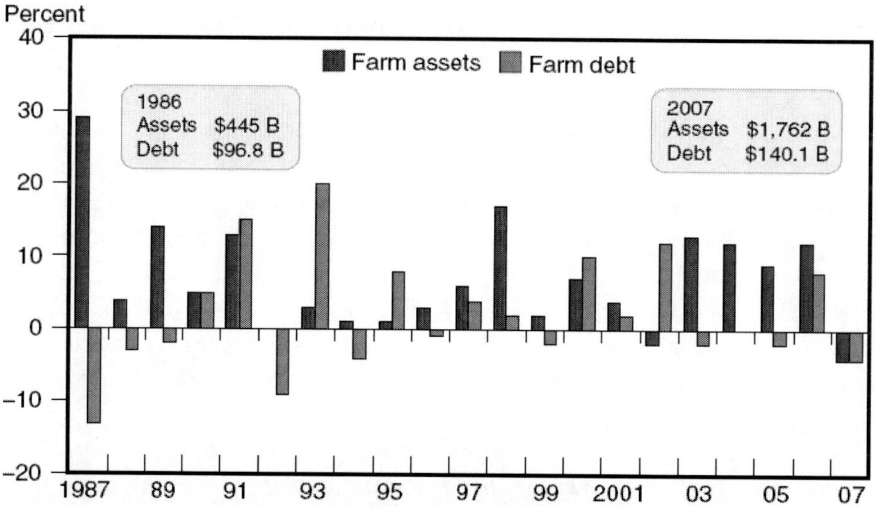

Source: Agricultural Resource Management Survey and Farm Costs and Returns Survey, USDA, National Agricultural Statistics Service and Economic Research Service.

Figure 9. Growth in farm business assets and debt, 1987-2007.

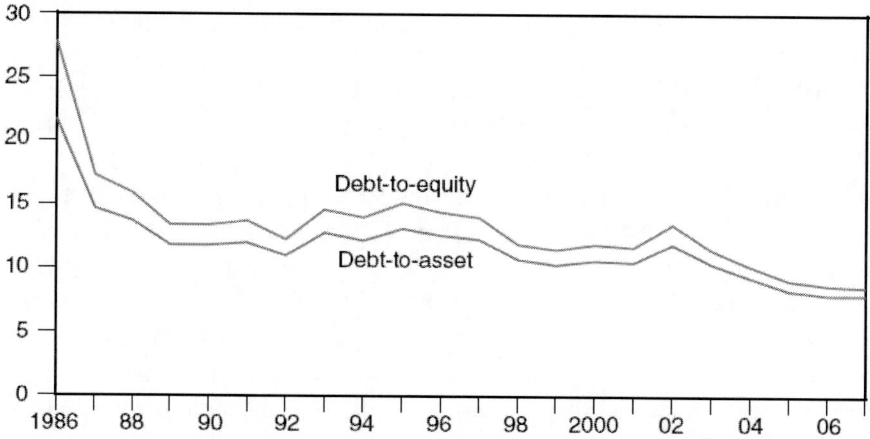

Source: Agricultural Resource Management Survey and Farm Costs and Returns Survey, USDA, National Agricultural Statistics Service and Economic Research Service.

Figure 10. Farm business debt-to-asset and debt-to-equity ratios, 1986-2007.

Debt Declines Relative to the Income and Cash-Flow Earned by Stakeholders in U.S. Agriculture

While the rise in sectorwide asset values, particularly for farmland, substantially enhanced the financial position of U.S. agriculture, it is earnings and funds available to agricultural stakeholders, not assets or equity, that service farm debt. Lenders and borrowers alike learned hard lessons during the 1980s when loans based on collateral proved problematic as income and land values fell from pre-crisis highs. By the mid-1980s, lower prices for commodities, particularly crops, and rising input costs--especially the costs of servicing record high amounts of debt--led to the bankruptcy of thousands of farms and the failure of hundreds of farm lenders.

Nominal farm earnings, as measured by net income, and cash availability, as measured by net cash income, have trended upward since the late 1980s (Figure 11). Even after adjusting for inflation, net farm income rose to challenge the levels earned three to four decades ago. With the drawdown in net farm income projected for 2009, net farm income adjusted for inflation will likely fall below $50 billion (in 2000 dollars) for only the third time since the 1980s. Cash income will also be at its lowest inflation-adjusted level since the early 1980s. Still, income gains over the last decade mean that sectorwide debt use relative to net cash income dropped from a ratio of 5 or more in the 1980s to less than 3 for most of the last 20 years (Figure 12). In 2009, the sectorwide debt use is expected to remain at near-record levels, but net farm income is projected to fall due to higher input costs and lower commodity prices, particularly for livestock. At 3. 4 times net cash income in 2009, debt burden will have been higher in only one other year (3. 45 in 2002) since 1985.

Net cash flow measures the cash resources available to farm sector stakeholders for investment and to service debt. It differs from net cash income in that it accounts for both internal and external sources of funds available to stakeholders; net cash income only accounts for the cash earned from the production and sale of farm goods and services. Cash flow is determined by net cash income along with changes in farm business debt, financial asset values, net rents, interest expenses, and expenditures on capital items (see box, "Net Cash Flow").

Net cash income has trended upward since the mid-1980s, with nominal records established in 2004 and again in 2008. Changes in sectorwide debt use and asset values have been largely positive, as have net rents paid to landlords. As a result, net cash flow expanded over the last 20 years both in absolute terms and relative to debt owed by agricultural stakeholders. Debt relative to net cash flow surged in 2 years, 2000 and 2002, when net cash income fell to levels earned in the mid-1980s and early 1990s while debt remained largely on an upward trend (Figure 13). Even with the reduction in cash flow projected for 2009, the ratio of debt to net cash flow is projected to be about 3. 1. Agriculture's stakeholders, as a whole, have had more cash available to pay off debt in most years since the early 1990s than was the case in the mid-1980s.

Net cash flow (after interest expenses) is defined as:

Net cash income

+ change in farm business debt
+ net change in other financial assets
+ net rent to non-operator landlords (excluding capital consumption)
- capital expenditures (excluding operator dwellings)
- interest expenses (excluding operator dwellings).

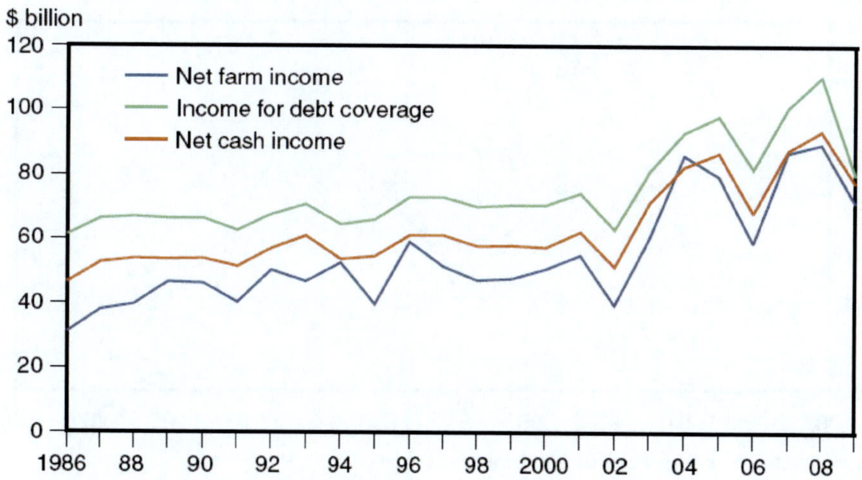

Source: USDA, Economic Research Service.

Figure 11. U.S. farm sector income and net cash income, 1986-2009f.

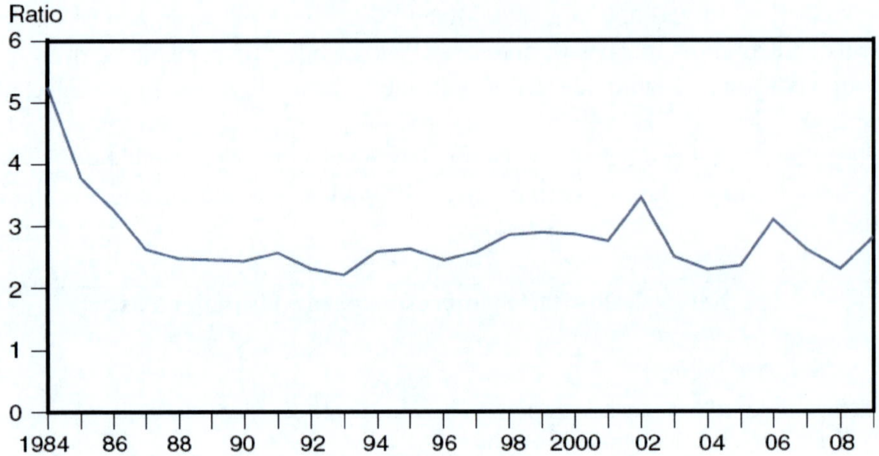

Source: USDA, Economic Research Service.

Figure 12. U.S. farm sector debt-to-net-cash-income ratio, 1984-2009f.

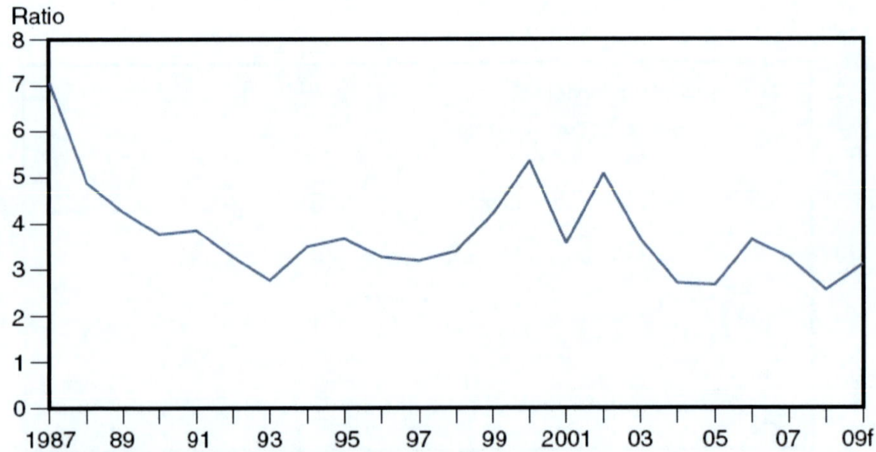

Source: USDA, Economic Research Service.

Figure 13. Farm sector debt/net cash flow 1987-2009f.

Debt Also Declines Relative to Cash Income Earned by Farm Businesses

The trends in debt use and earnings among farm businesses roughly mirror farming as a whole, with the percentage increase in the level of cash earnings exceeding the increase in the level of debt by a wide margin. Net cash income earned by farm businesses, as measured from farmers' survey responses, increased almost four-fold during the past two decades, rising from about $13 billion in 1986 to nearly $49 billion in 2007. [7] Meanwhile, farm business debt reported by farmers for their businesses increased by a factor of about 1. 5 over the same period. As a result, debt in relation to net cash income earned across all farm businesses dropped from 7. 5 times income in 1986 to 2. 9 times income in 2007 (Figure 14).

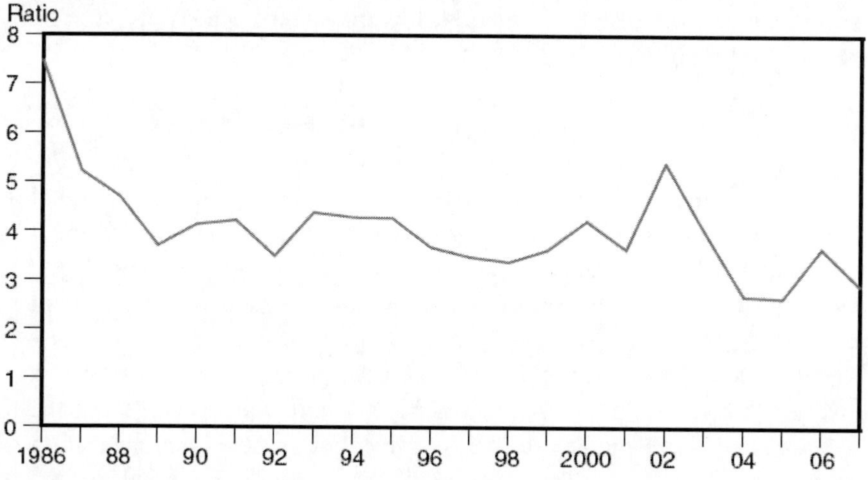

Source: Agricultural Resource Management Survey and Farm Costs and Returns Survey, USDA, National Agricultural Statistics Service and Economic Research Service.

Figure 14. Debt owed in relation to net cash income, 1986-2007 Ratio.

Debt Repayment Capacity Utilization Down in U.S. Agriculture Sector

Debt repayment capacity can be defined as the maximum amount of debt that can be supported by net cash income available for loan repayment (see box, "Components of sectorwide DRCU calculations"). At the farm-sector level, debt repayment capacity utilization (DRCU)[8] is the ratio of farm stakeholders', including operators', farm debt to the maximum feasible debt in any given year based on current earnings of the sector.

At the sector level, DRCU is a measure of the ability of farm stakeholders, including operators, to repay their debt over time through the production and sale of farm products and services. DRCU indicates the potential for farm repayment problems, given farm earnings and interest rates on debt owed by the sector (Figure 15). Overall, the relationship between debt owed and debt levels that could be supported from current earnings suggests that farm sector asset owners have maintained a sizeable repayment cushion since the crisis years of the 1980s. Falling interest rates and rising incomes have supported the repayment cushion. Repayment capacity is projected to shrink in 2009. Despite little change in interest rates and nominal farm debt levels, a decrease in farm income will result in higher debt repayment capacity use for farm stakeholders (Figure 16).

Components of sectorwide DRCU calculations

Income for Debt Coverage = Net farm income + interest on capital debt[1] *Debt Repayment* = Principal and interest on capital debt + capital lease payments *Total Debt Coverage Ratio* = Income for debt coverage / debt repayment *Debt Coverage Margin* = Income for debt coverage – debt payment

Minimum debt coverage ratio = lender requirement; based on a coverage ratio of 1. 25 which requires that no more than 80 percent of the loan applicant's income be used for repayment of principal and interest on loans.

Maximum Loan Payment = Income for debt coverage / minimum debt coverage ratio

Debt Repayment Capacity = Maximum loan payment x $(1-(1+r)^{-n})/r$, where $(1-(1+r)^{-n}/r$ = present value of an annuity of $1, at r percent for n periods (7 years).

Debt Repayment Capacity Utilization = Debt / debt repayment capacity.

[1] Interest payments (deducted from net farm income as a cost of production) are added back in to measure all of current farm income available for debt repayment.

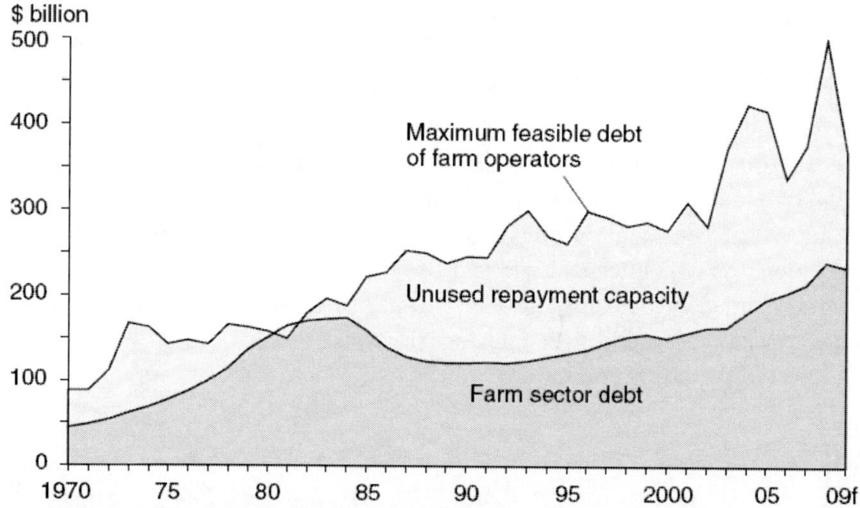

2009 forecast.

Source: USDA, Economic Research Service.

Figure 15. Farm sector debt and repayment capacity, 1970-2009f.

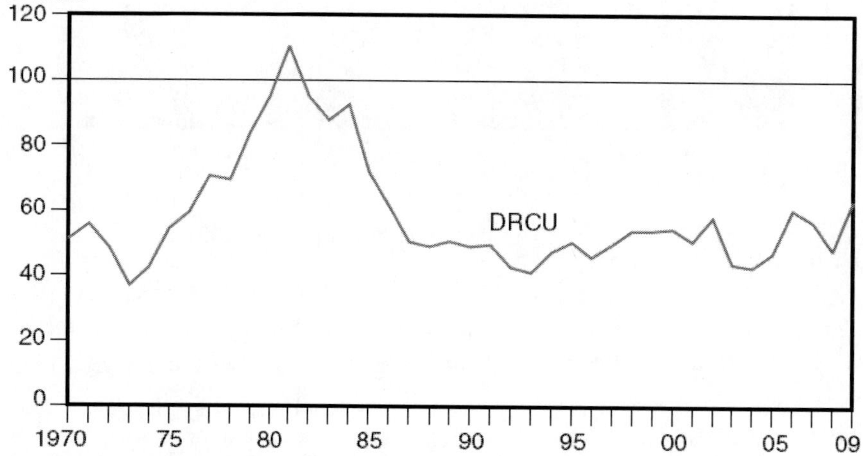

Note: 2008 and 2009 forecast.

Source: USDA, Economic Research Service.

Figure 16. Farm sector debt repayment capacity utilization (DRCU), 1970-2009f.

Debt Repayment Capacity Use Varies Over Time at the Farm Level

Farmers' use of their farm's debt carrying capacity has declined in recent years. In 2007, debt repayment capacity use (DRCU) for all farm businesses (see box, "Components of DRCU calculations for farm businesses") stood at less than 20 percent, while farms with debt outstanding used about 41 percent of their debt repayment capacity (Figure 17). DRCU fell both for all farms and for farms with debt over the decade. Despite mounting debt in recent years, rising farm incomes and lower interest rates--plus fewer farmers using debt--have lowered the utilization ratio.

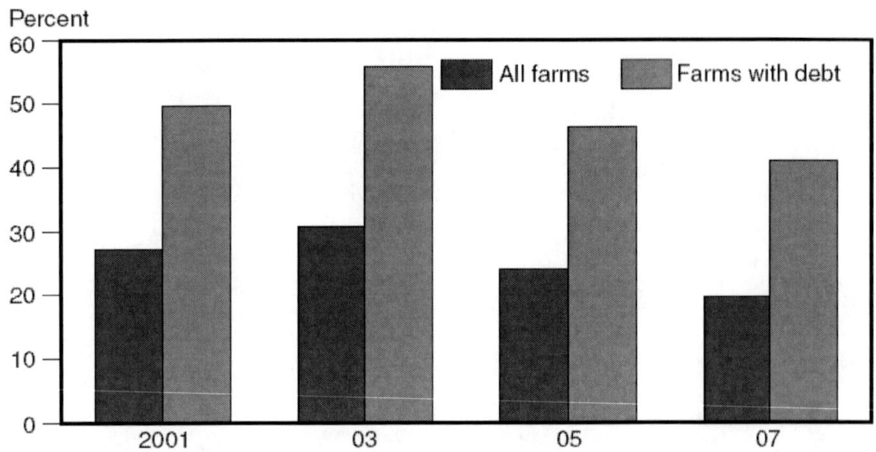

Source: Agricultural Resource Management Survey.

Figure 17. Debt repayment capacity utilization at the farm level, 2001-07.

While DRCU has varied over time, use of debt repayment capacity also varies considerably across farm size categories (Figure 18). Larger farms, those with $5 million or more in annual sales, used nearly 37 percent of their debt repayment capacity in 2007. Larger farms are more capital intensive than smaller farms and tend to carry more debt on their balance sheet. Smaller farms tended to have much lower utilization numbers in 2007. DRCU was less across all farm size groups in 2007 than in 2001.

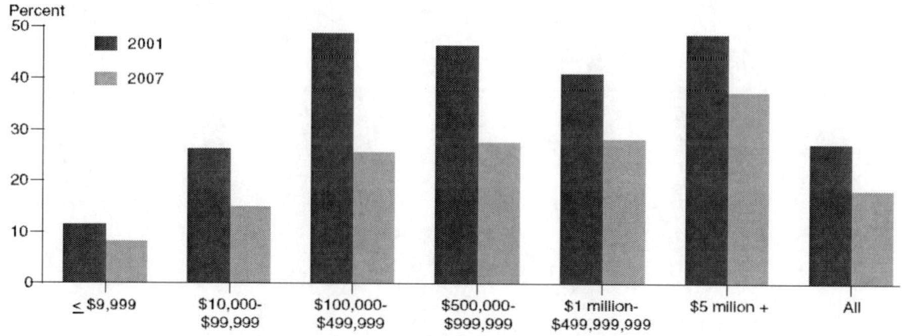

Source: USDA, Agricultural Resource Management Survey.

Figure 18. Debt repayment capacity utilization by farm size, 2001 and 2007.

Debt repayment capacity also varies considerably across farm types (Figure 19). Poultry operations had the highest DRCU in 2007 (over 60 percent). These operations use high levels of borrowed capital to finance contract operations. Poultry is followed by dairy and hog farms. Cash grains also had a fairly high DRCU in 2007—over 25 percent. DRCU values fell between 2001 and 2007 for some types of operations, such as cash grain and soybeans, but increased for poultry and dairy. DRCU values also vary by region (Figure 20). Geographical variations in financial markets and types of farms tend to drive these differences. The highest DRCU values for 2007 were found in the Lake States, Northeast, Pacific, and Northern Plains regions. The lowest DRCU in 2007 was in the Southern Plains. Debt repayment capacity utilization was lower in most regions in 2007 compared to 2001—Appalachia and the Southeast were exceptions.

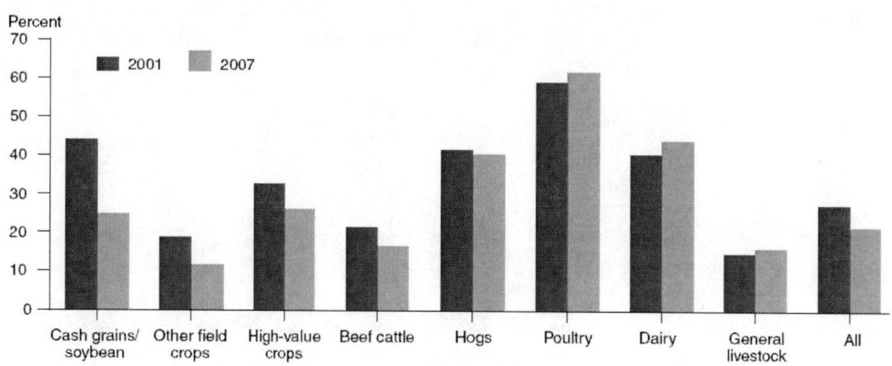

Source: USDA, Agricultural Resource Management Survey.

Figure 19. Debt repayment capacity utilization by farm typology, 2001 and 2007.

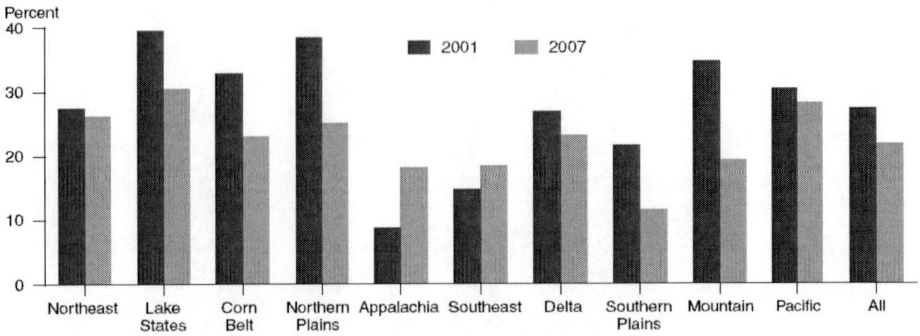

Source: USDA, Agricultural Resource Management Survey.

Figure 20. Debt repayment capacity utilization by farm region, 2001 and 2007.

Applying a minimum debt coverage ratio requirement to any farm operation permits us to determine the maximum amount of debt that can be repaid from any level of income. ERS has traditionally used a total debt service ratio of 1.2:1. At this point, a farm would owe 20 percent more debt than could be serviced with annual income (Ryan and Morehart, 1992). Farms with debt repayment capacity use above 1.2 may have difficulty meeting debt service obligations from current farm household income.

The share of farms with DRCU values over 1.2 was nearly 5 percentage points, or more than a fifth, lower in 2007 than in 2001 (Figure 21). In addition, the level of debt held by these potentially distressed farms was over 7 percentage points lower in 2007 than it was in 2001. This decrease parallels overall decreases in the DRCU of farm businesses.

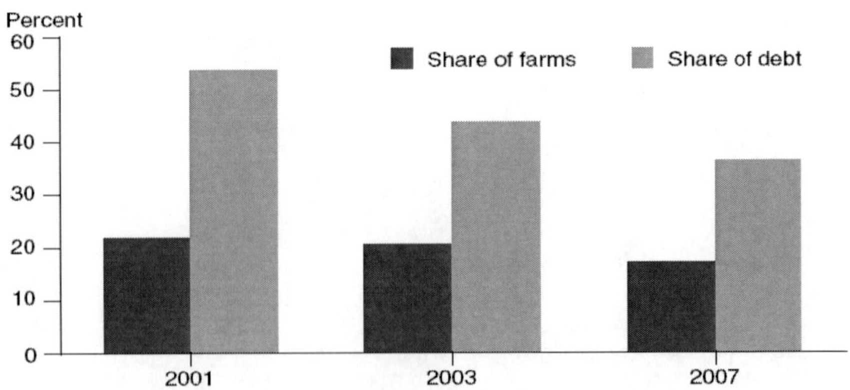

Source: USDA, Agricultural Resource Management Survey.

Figure 21. Share of farm businesses with a DRCU over 1.2, selected years, 2001-07.

Components of DRCU calculation for farm business

Income for Debt Coverage = Net farm income + Depreciation + Interest on capital debt + Capital lease payments – Income taxes

Off-farm income, living expenses, and income taxes were excluded from the computation of income for debt coverage in the preliminary analysis presented here

Debt Repayment = Principal and interest on capital debt + Capital lease payments

Total Debt Coverage Ratio = Income for debt coverage / Debt repayment

Debt Coverage Margin = Income for debt coverage – Debt payment

Maximum Loan Payment = Income for debt coverage / Minimum debt coverage ratio

Debt Repayment Capacity = Maximum loan payment x $(1-(1+r)^{-n})/r$, where $(1-(1+r)^{-n}/r$ = present value of an annuity of \$1, at r percent for n periods (7 years).

Debt Repayment Capacity Utilization = Debt / Debt repayment capacity.

WHICH FARMS HOLD DEBT?

- Thirty-one percent of farms held debt in 2007, compared to 60 percent in 1986.
- Debt is concentrated in larger farms, and in dairy, poultry, and hog farms.
- The Northern Plains, Corn Belt, and Lake States have the highest percentage of farms with debt.

Farmers' responses to annual ARMS survey questions about debt use indicate that the share of operators that finance business activities with debt capital has dropped over the past two decades (Figure 22). Overall, farms as individual businesses mirror changes in the farm sector as a whole, with debt comprising a smaller share of their capital structure. However, neither a sectorwide nor an aggregate farm business-level perspective about debt use relative to assets or income is sufficient to understand the debt-use landscape facing U.S. farms. Aggregate industry and "all-farm" views fail to indicate which farm operators use debt to finance their farm operations or the potential severity of financial distress within farming. Sector-level data, for example, cannot be used to align who holds debt with who owns assets and earns income (see Appendix).

Likewise, while the financial position of farms as businesses across production agriculture could appear favorable, a misalignment of debt and debt service obligations with income, assets, and equity may exist at the firm level. Farmers who owe debt could be substantially different from farmers that are generating positive earnings and cash flows. Moreover, farmers that owe debt may differ from farmers that have substantial asset and equity positions in their businesses.

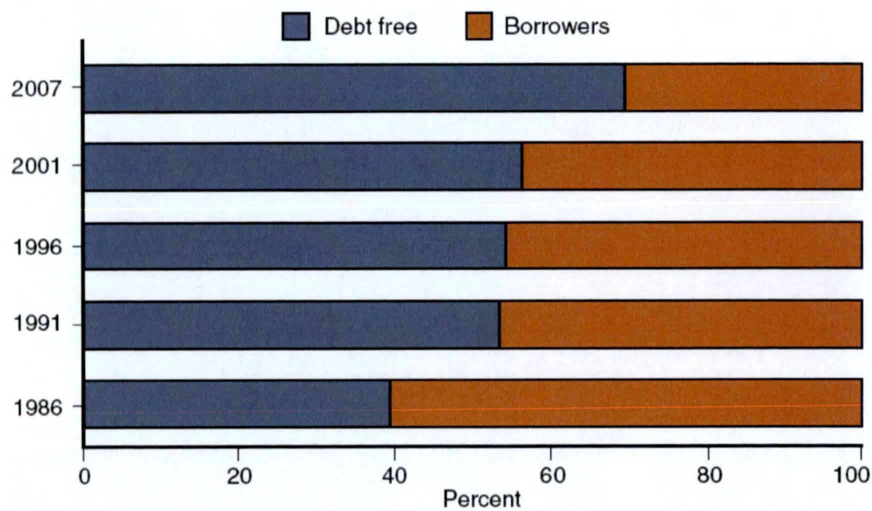

*Based on debt outstanding at year's end.

Source: Agricultural Resource Management Survey and Farm Costs and Returns Survey,

USDA, National Agricultural Statistics Service and Economic Research Service.

Figure 22. Farm operator debt use, selected years, 1986-2007*.

Sector-level data could mask highly diverse financial experiences among farms and among lenders, as was apparent during the 1980s farm crisis (Johnson and Morehart, 1987). Farm-level data can help identify those farmers unable to access credit markets without government-based loan guarantees.[9] These guarantee programs shift some of the risks associated with farm lending from lenders to government agencies.

Distribution of Debt Among Farm Businesses

Large farm businesses, as measured by value of sales, more frequently report use of debt than smaller farms (Figure 23). Nationally, 31 percent of farms owed debt at year-end 2007. Not only do larger farm businesses more frequently use debt, the average amount of debt, per farm, that is acquired by these businesses is also substantially larger. For example, in 2007, the average amount of debt carried at year-end rose from about $94,000 for farms with sales of $100,000-$250,000 to $319,000 for farms with sales of $500,000-$999,999 and to $2. 8 million for farms with sales of $5 million or more. Although smaller farms are more numerous, the higher frequency of debt use by large farms and their greater debt load results in debt being concentrated among larger farm businesses.

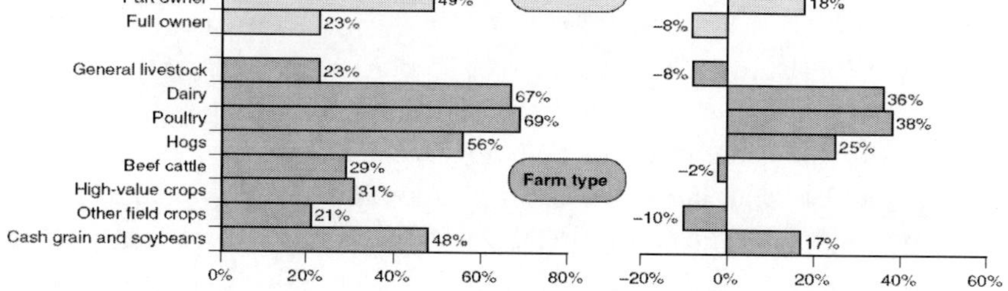

Source: Agricultural Resource Management Survey, USDA, National Agricultural Statistics Service and Economic Research Service.

Figure 23. Use of farm business debt in 2007, by farm typology.

Data reported by farmers for 2007 showed that the 5. 4 percent of farms with sales over $500,000 owed about 46 percent while the 2 percent of farms with sales over $1 million owed 29 percent of farm business debt (Table 1, p. 29).

Cash expenditures for farm inputs have risen from $110 billion in the 1980s to $238 billion in 2007. Farmers' cash expenses are forecast to rise by another $10 billion by the end of 2009. Meanwhile, expenditures for capital items such as machinery, equipment, or structures such as housing for hogs, poultry, or greenhouse products have also more than doubled since the 1980s. Expenditures for operating inputs and capital items, like sales, tend to be concentrated among larger farm businesses. For example, in 2007, the 5. 4 percent of farms with sales over $500,000 accounted for 60 percent of production input expenses, while the largest 2 percent of farms--those with over $1 million in annual sales—accounted for 44 percent of expenses. Given the expenses of larger farm businesses, it is not surprising that debt use also tends to be centered on these farms. The sheer volume of inputs needed to generate farm products and services results in large farms having greater needs for capital, including debt capital, than smaller farm businesses.

Larger farms are also generally more dependent on earnings from the farm business for their household income than are operators of smaller farms. Small farms (less than $250,000 in annual sales), which make up the vast majority of farm operations, are more dependent on off-farm sources of income—such as off-farm jobs, pensions, or retirement savings—for household expenses. Off-farm sources of income, whether from current earnings or from savings and investments, may reduce the need to use debt financing on many small farm operations.

For farms with sales over $500,000, over two-thirds reported owing debt at year-end 2007 (Figure 24). This is much higher than the debt use of farms in the smaller sales classes. Larger farm businesses have consistently used more debt since the 1980s. In 1986, for example, 86 percent of farms with sales over $500,000 reported debt while 43 percent of farms with sales less than $10,000 had debt. While the share of farms with debt has declined for all sales classes, the relationship between large and small farm operations has not changed—in 2007, farms with sales over $500,000 accounted for 72 percent of farm business debt, while farms with under $10,000 in sales held less than 20 percent.

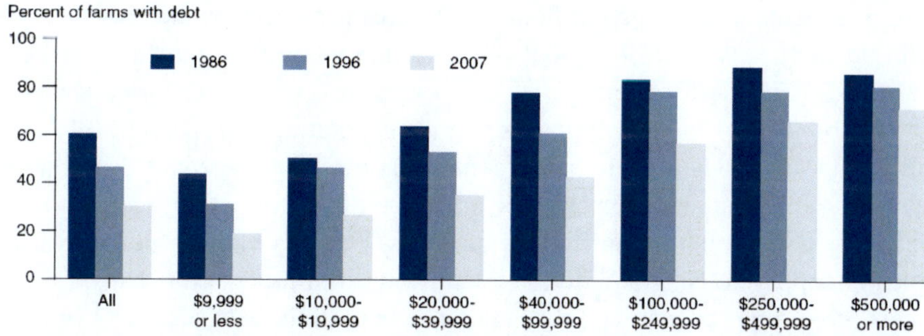

Source: Agricultural Resource Management Survey and Farm Costs and Returns Survey, USDA, National Agricultural Statistics Service, and Economic Research Service.

Figure 24. Use of farm business debt by sales class, selected years, 1986-2007.

The average size of a farm, in acres operated, with no year-end debt was 290 acres in 2007; the average size of a farm reporting debt was 684 acres (Figure 25). Businesses that used debt financing also had a larger percentage of rented property than operations functioning without debt. Farmers that did not have debt payable at year-end were much more likely to be full owners than were farmers who owed debt.

Capital needs vary significantly by type of farm business as measured by the predominant commodity, or group of commodities, produced by the business. Dairy, hog, specialty crop (fruit or vegetable), cotton, rice, and cash grain farms produce a larger share of the total value of production and use a larger than proportionate share of inputs, as reflected in annual cash expenses. These farms also have a much larger asset base than all farms, on average. General cash grain and corn farms operate more acres, while specialty crop and dairy farm businesses have a larger value of assets per acre operated. On the other hand, general crop and livestock operations account for relatively small amounts of output relative to the share of farms they represent.

Given inputs used and assets owned, it is not surprising that the highest average amount of debt is reported by dairy producers and poultry growers (over $226,000, on average, in 2007), followed by hog, general cash grain, and corn producers. These farm types were also the most likely to report year-end debt.

The largest deviation between the reported share of farms with debt and the share of farm debt occurred for dairy businesses, followed by corn and general cash grain operators. Dairy operations accounted for only 2. 9 percent of all farms but owed 13. 3 percent of reported farm-level debt. Corn farms were 6. 2 percent of farms but held 13. 2 percent of debt, while general cash grain businesses were 3. 9 percent of farms and owed 9. 4 percent of debt at year-end 2007. Poultry operations were next at 1. 8 percent of farms and 6. 4 percent of debt. Poultry farms reported generating 10 percent of total production value when value under contract is taken into account. But a large share of the output and expenses used in poultry production accrue to the contractor with which the farm does business. Farmers that run poultry farms typically supply housing and other structures used in production. Thus, having almost three times as many poultry operators reporting real estate debt as non-real estate debt is consistent with how these farms operate. Corn and general cash grain farms also have a slightly higher percentage of farmers reporting real estate loans. For dairy, a larger share reported non-real estate loans at year-end 2007, and this is probably associated with purchased feed and livestock for use in the dairy enterprise.

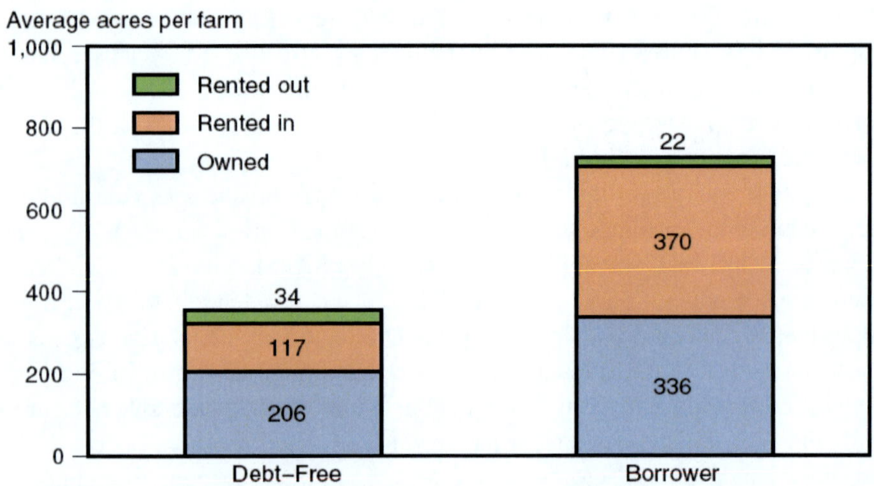

Source: Agricultural Resource Management Survey and Farm Costs and Returns Survey, USDA, National Agricultural Statistics Service and Economic Research Service.

Figure 25. Farm acreage by farm operator borrowing class and tenure, 2007 Average acres per farm.

At the other end of the spectrum, general crop farms accounted for 21 percent of farms and 5. 6 percent of debt at year-end 2007, while general livestock accounted for about 22 percent of farms and 11 percent of debt. Only about one in five operators of these farms reported owing debt at year-end

2007. Nearly three-quarters of the operators of general crop/livestock businesses report working off-farm or being inactive in the work force. Thus, they may be at a stage of life where farm debt is paid down or have access to funds from off-farm jobs or prior investments that can be used to fund current farm activities.

Debt use in the Northern Plains, Lake States, and Corn Belt is higher than the national mean, with the share of farms reporting debt at year-end 2007 10 to 14 percentage points higher than for farms nationwide. The share of farms reporting debt use was highest in the Northern Plains, at 45 percent, followed by the Lake States at 38 percent (Figure 26). The Corn Belt accounted for nearly 21 percent of farm debt and, together with the Northern Plains and Lake States, 47 percent of all farm-based debt. The Southeast had the smallest share of farms with reported debt use at 18 percent of farms.

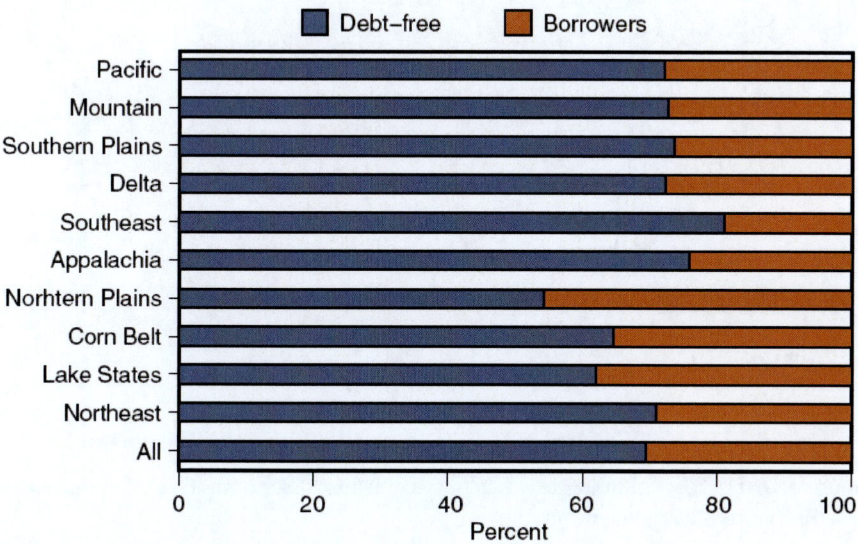

Source: Agricultural Resource Management Survey, USDA, National Agricultural Statistics Service and Economic Research Service.

Figure 26. Farm business debt use in 2007, by region.

Geospatial tools allow us to examine the intensity of farm-level debt use on a much more granular basis than the broad production regions discussed above. The highest concentration of farm business debt in 2007 was in the Corn Belt, the Southeast, the Mississippi Valley, the Northern Plains, and the Mid-Atlantic (Figure 27). These are all areas that feature a larger than proportionate share of grain, hog, poultry, and dairy operations, which are heavy users of debt capital.

A traditional farm is typically portrayed as consisting of a single individual or family that owns the operation, makes management decisions, and runs day-to-day operations (Boehlje and Erickson, 2007). These traditional farmers are presumed to largely finance their operations through retained earnings or by borrowing modest amounts from lenders or family members. Employees are usually family members or neighbors, and when the primary operator retires or dies, the farm is usually transitioned to the next generation of the family or sold.

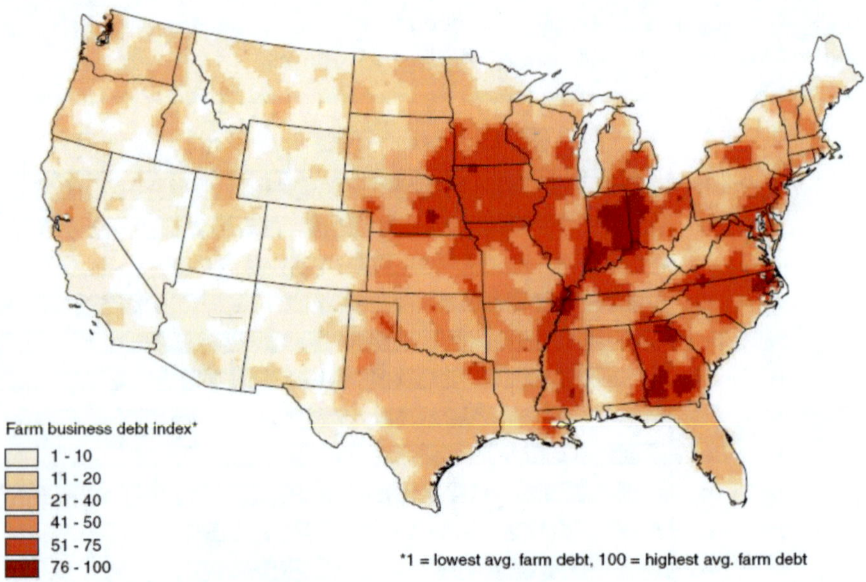

Source: USDA, Economic Research Service using data from USDA's Agricultural Resource Management Survey.

Figure 27. The Corn Belt, Northern Plains, and South had greater debt use in 2007.

Many 21st century farms do not fit this traditional farm model. Some operations have multiple owners, which may include non-family members. Managers who oversee daily operations may not be related to farm owners. The farm may be incorporated and have a board of directors that dictates strategic and operational decisions for the business. These operations may seek financing from a wide variety of avenues, including investors or stockholders as well as traditional lenders. Data reported by farm operators for 2007 show that farms with multiple owners and multiple operators tend to have a larger than proportionate share of farms with debt (Figure 28). Multiple owners and operators increase the number of individuals with whom lenders may need to interact (Klinefelter and Penson, 2005). Likewise, identifying responsible parties for loan service obligations may become more difficult.

Concentration of Debt Among Farms

The most recent Census of Agriculture, conducted for the 2007 calendar year, reported that 30. 3 percent of farms had interest expenses. The comparable statistic for the previous census, concluded 5 years earlier, was 35. 6 percent.[10] At 31 percent, the share of farms reporting debt at year end 2007 in ARMS was similar to the 30. 3 percent of farms that reported interest expenses in the Census. Both show that a smaller share of farms reported using debt at year-end 2007 than at any time in the past two decades (Figure 29).

Even though a smaller proportion of farms rely on debt than in the past, some farms remain highly leveraged. The 2007 ARMS indicates that 0. 5 percent of farms owed more debt than they had assets (table 1), similar to the level in 1991. Farms with more debt than assets in 2007 owed 5. 5 percent of total farm business debt, versus 2. 4 percent in 1991.

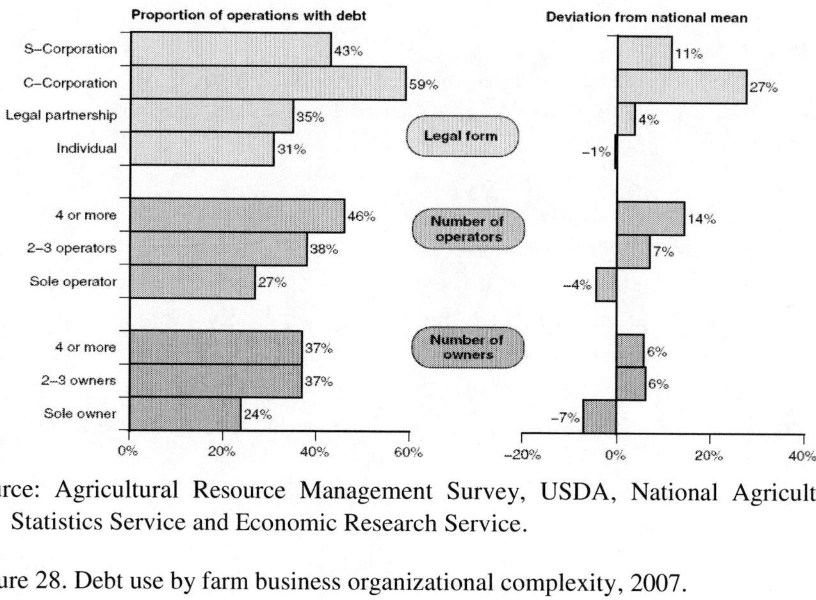

Source: Agricultural Resource Management Survey, USDA, National Agricultural Statistics Service and Economic Research Service.

Figure 28. Debt use by farm business organizational complexity, 2007.

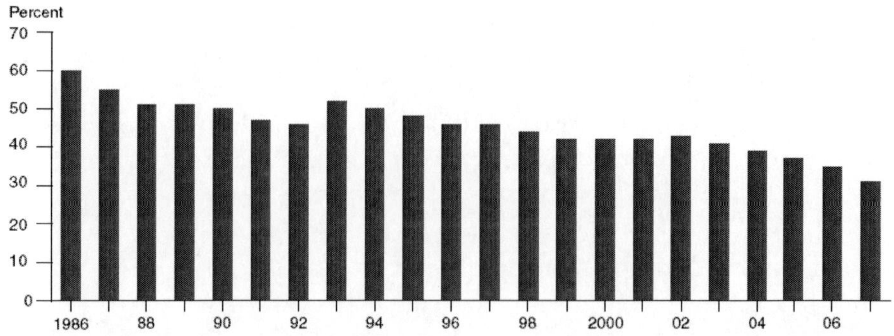

Source: Agricultural Resource Management Survey, USDA, National Agricultural Statistics Service and Economic Research Service.

Figure 29. Share of farm businesses that report inter-year use of business debt, 1986-2007.

Table 1. Distribution of farms and debt by leverage class, 1991 and 2007

	No Debt		0.00 to 0.40		0.41 to 0.70		0.71 to 1.00		Over 1.00	
	1991	2007	1991	2007	1991	2007	1991	2007	1991	2007
% farms	59.8	68.8	35.3	25.5	3.8	4.3	0.6	1.0	0.5	0.5
% debt	-	-	73.8	63.4	20.2	24.0	3.5	7.0	2.4	5.5
ROA[1]	0.2	0.3	0.2	3.2	2.2	5.5	3.0	7.3	-6.0	11.9
OPM[2]	1.9	2.6	1.2	15.3	6.3	13.9	5.5	12.5	-11.4	16.5

[1]Return on assets.

[2]Operating profit margin.

Source: Agricultural Resource Management Survey and Farm Costs and Returns Survey, USDA, National Agricultural Statistics Service and Economic Research Service.

Although the share of highly leveraged farms is about the same today as it was in 1991, one fundamental difference is the profitability of these highly leveraged farms. Using return on assets and operating profit margin as measures of financial performance, farms were generally more profitable in 2007 than they were in 1991. Also, the more highly leveraged operations generated greater returns on their investment in 2007 than did farms with less debt relative to assets—a marked change from the financial performance picture in 1991.

Farms that either held debt equal to 71-100 percent of asset values or that were technically insolvent (with debt levels in excess of the current market value of assets) have decreased since the 1980s and include all sizes of farms

(Figure 30 and 31). [11] Poultry and high-value crop farms had a larger than proportional share of insolvent farms in 2007. Farms with debt equal to 71-100-percent of asset values included a more than proportionate share of hog, dairy, and poultry operations. General livestock farms, which tend to be among the smallest farms both in terms of the acreage operated and value of production, also reported a larger than proportionate share of highly leveraged and technically insolvent farms in 2007. Overall, general livestock farms accounted for more than one in four insolvent farms; together with high-value crop operations, they accounted for over half.

Nearly three-fourths of farms with sales of $500,000 or more reported debt, compared with well under half of farms with sales less than $100,000 in annual sales (Figure 31). While farms with sales over $500,000 accounted for just over 5 percent of all farms, they accounted for about 14 percent of farms with debt and held 46 percent of farm debt at year-end 2007.

To further assess the degree of debt concentration, farms were ordered by decile groupings to enable measurement of the fewest number of farms that held 50, 25, and 10 percent of debt at different points in time over the past 20 years (table 2). In 1991, 50 percent of farm business debt was held by 23 percent of farm operators. By 2007, this proportion of debt was held by 15 percent of farm operators. Between 1991 and 2007 the number of farms needed to account for half of farm business debt fell from over 488,000 to about 333,000 or nearly a third. About 67,000 farms were needed to account for 10 percent of farm-level debt in 2007, down from nearly 98,000 farms in 1991. USDA surveys began to track farm-level debt in the 1980s, but the early surveys did not fully reflect the population of farms in U.S. agriculture, particularly small farms. Even so, the data still show an increasing concentration of debt on fewer farms.

For farms with debt, the gini coefficient, which measures the dispersion of debt among farm businesses, remained relatively flat (Figure 32). This suggests that the composition of farms that owe debt has remained relatively stable. When the dispersion of debt is examined across all farms, however, the gini coefficient increases by about 10 percentage points, from 79 in 1986 to 90 in 2007, indicating that debt use has become more concentrated.

Table 2. Concentration of U.S. farm debt in selected years, 1986-2007

Item	1986	1991	1996	2001	2006	2007
Top 50 percent of debt						
Number	458,483	488,318	468,002	459,078	366,401	333,453
Percentage	30.2	23.3	23.1	21.4	17.6	15.2
Top 25 percent of debt						
Number	226,438	250,804	233,946	224,478	184,418	167,448
Percentage	14.9	11.9	11.6	10.4	8.9	7.6
Top 10 percent of debt						
Number	90,562	97,712	93,520	90,298	75,341	66,723
Percentage	6.0	4.7	4.6	4.2	3.6	3.0

Source: Agricultural Resource Management Survey and Farm Costs and Returns Survey, USDA, National Agricultural Statistics Service and Economic Research Service.

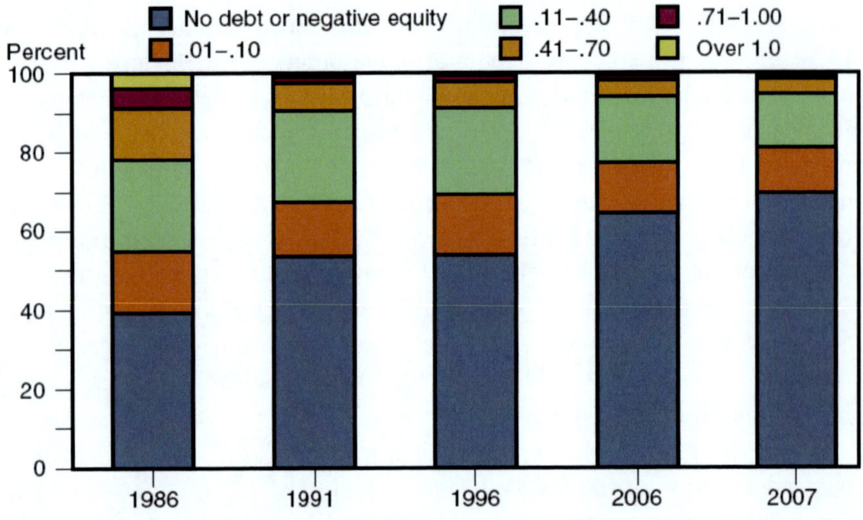

Source: Agricultural Resource Management Survey, USDA, National Agricultural Statistics Service and Economic Research Service.

Figure 30. Distribution of farms by debt-to-asset ratio, selected years, 1986-2007.

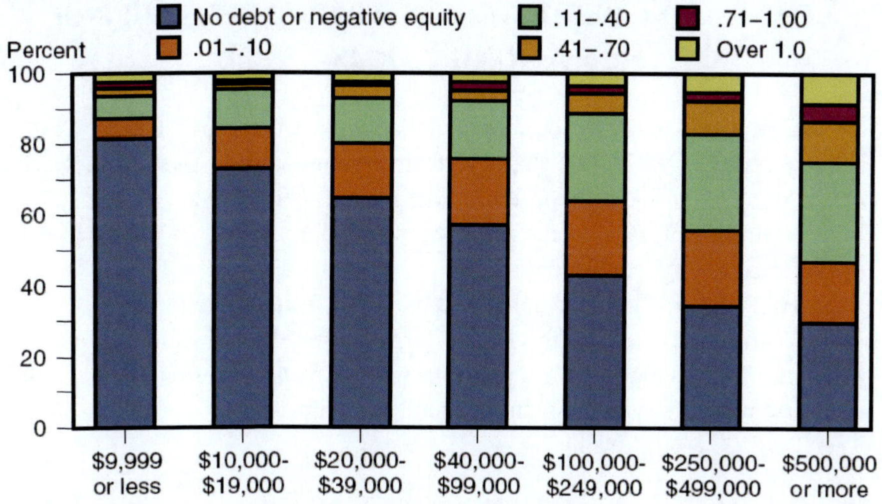

Source: Agricultural Resource Management Survey, USDA, National Agricultural Statistics Service and Economic Research Service.

Figure 31. Distribution of farms by economic size of farms and debt-to-asset ratio, 2007.

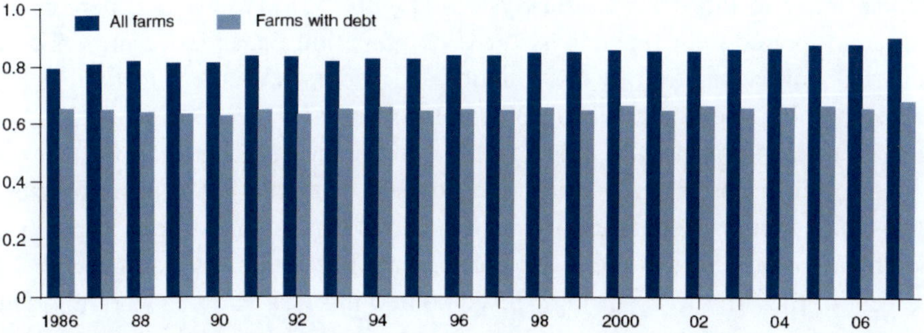

Source: Agricultural Resource Management Survey, USDA, National Agricultural Statistics Service and Economic Research Service.

Figure 32. Gini coefficients of debt for all farms and for farms that report debt use, 1986-2007.

LOANS AND CREDIT ACCESS APPROACHES DIFFER AMONG FARMS

- Compared to 1998, commercial banks and the Farm Credit System account for a higher share of farm lending, while the Farm Service Agency and individuals and others have lower shares.
- Farm operators' choices and access to different types of credit vary by farm size, type, and region.
- Half of farms that use debt have one loan from one lender.
- While real estate is the single largest type of loan and the primary purpose for debt, farm operators with debt were found to frequently use multiple types of loans for multiple purposes.

Farmers Secure Debt Financing From Commercial, Government, and Individual Sources

Of the 686,000 farm operators that reported owing debt at year-end 2007, 365,000 or 53 percent reported obtaining loans only from commercial banks, while 13 percent reported owing debt only to individuals and others and 11 percent only to the Farm Credit System (Figure 33). Twenty-two percent of farmers reported debt financing from a combination of lenders. Farmers that reported borrowing from a combination of lenders tended to operate larger farms in 2007, averaging over 1,130 acres per farm (66 percent more acres, on average, than all farms with debt and 175 percent larger than all farms).

Overall, farms that reported owing debt at year-end 2007 span all sizes, types, and regions, regardless of lender. Farms that reported debt owed to a combination of lenders were disproportionately in larger sales classes, with 24 percent of these farms reporting over $500,000 in sales. Farmers who reported borrowing only from individuals and others or commercial banks were slightly more likely to have sales of less than $100,000 than all farmers who reported debt (Figure 34). Cash grain, beef, and dairy operations accounted for over 63 percent of farmers who reported a combination of lenders. Thus, these farm types were not only proportionately more likely than other farms to owe debt at year-end, they were more likely to have acquired this debt from multiple lenders. Debt, as reported by farm operators for their businesses, is heavily concentrated among three lender groups (Figure 35). Commercial banks, the Farm Credit System, and individuals together held 95 percent of the debt outstanding at year-end 2007. For the entire U.S. farm sector (which accounts for all stakeholders engaged in farming), these lenders accounted for 92 percent of debt owed in 2007. While the total share of debt is similar for the three lender groups, the composition of debt holdings differs between the farm and sector-level estimates. Farmers report a larger share for banks while sectorwide estimates show a larger share of debt owed to both the Farm Credit System, and to individuals and others.

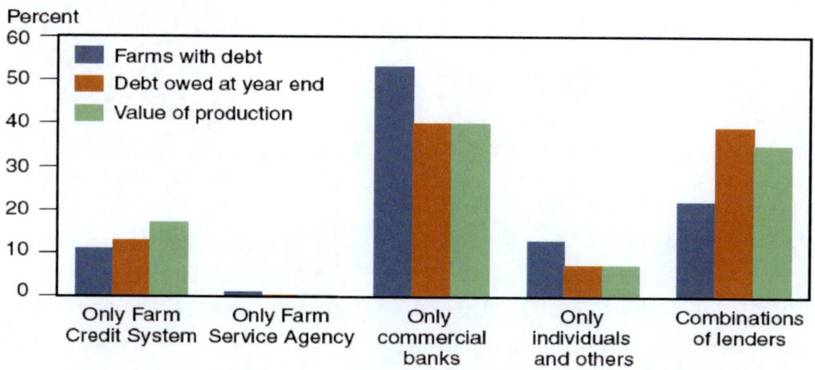

Source: USDA, Agricultural Resource Management Survey.

Figure 33. Farm operators' reporting of the source of debt owed at year end, 2007.

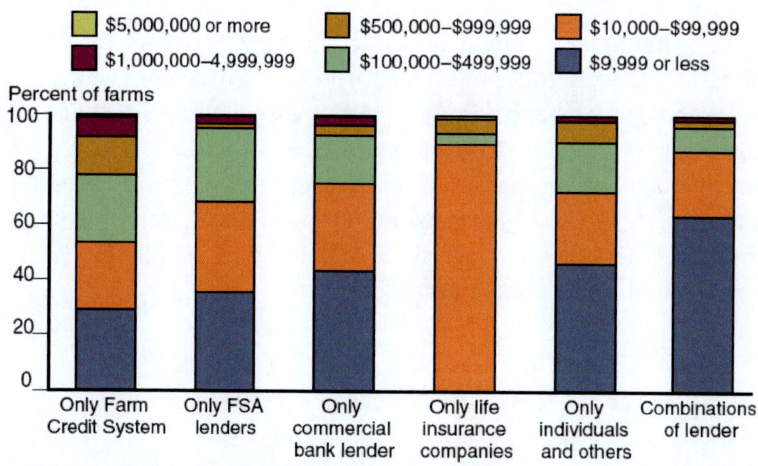

Source: Agricultural Resource Management Survey.

Figure 34. Distribution of farms by reported lender source for year-end debt and economic size of farm, 2007.

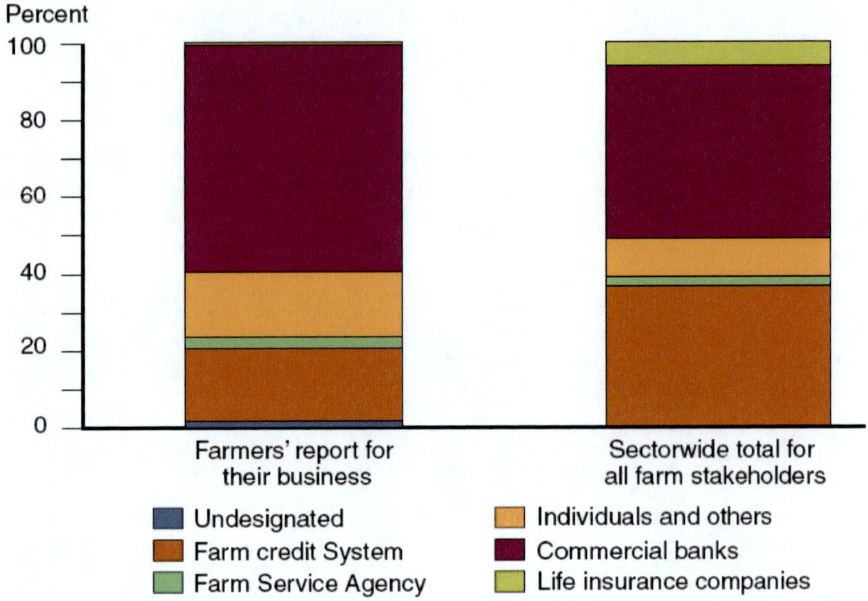

Source: Agricultural Resource Management Survey and Farm Sector Balance Sheet for U.S. agriculture.

Figure 35. Distribution of debt owed at year-end 2007 as reported by farmers for their businesses and for the U.S. farm sector.

Credit System, and individuals together held 95 percent of the debt outstanding at year-end 2007. For the entire U.S. farm sector (which accounts for all stakeholders engaged in farming), these lenders accounted for 92 percent of debt owed in 2007. While the total share of debt is similar for the three lender groups, the composition of debt holdings differs between the farm and sector-level estimates. Farmers report a larger share for banks while sectorwide estimates show a larger share of debt owed to both the Farm Credit System, and to individuals and others.

Operators Differ in How They Access Credit

At the end of 2007, 65 percent of farmers reported neither owing debt nor accessing a line of credit during the year to finance farm activities (Figure 36). Self-financed farms were the smallest farms in terms of land operated at an average of 258 acres. Farms with no debt at year-end, but with a line of credit that they used during the year, averaged 846 acres, while farms with both lines of credit and outstanding loan balances were the largest, averaging 968 acres.

Over 7 out of 10 debt-free farms reported less than $10,000 in sales. Farms that had an established line of credit against which they could draw funds (with or without an outstanding loan balance) were much more likely than other farms to have sales over $500,000 and especially over $1,000,000.

Farms that functioned without a line of credit or an outstanding loan were primarily beef cattle, general livestock, or general field crop farms. Dairy, poultry, hog, and cash grain and soybean producers were active users of both farm loans that extended across years and lines of credit. While farms in all regions used lines of credit and debt financing, farms in the Northern Plains, Lake States, and Corn Belt were more likely to make use of these financing options.

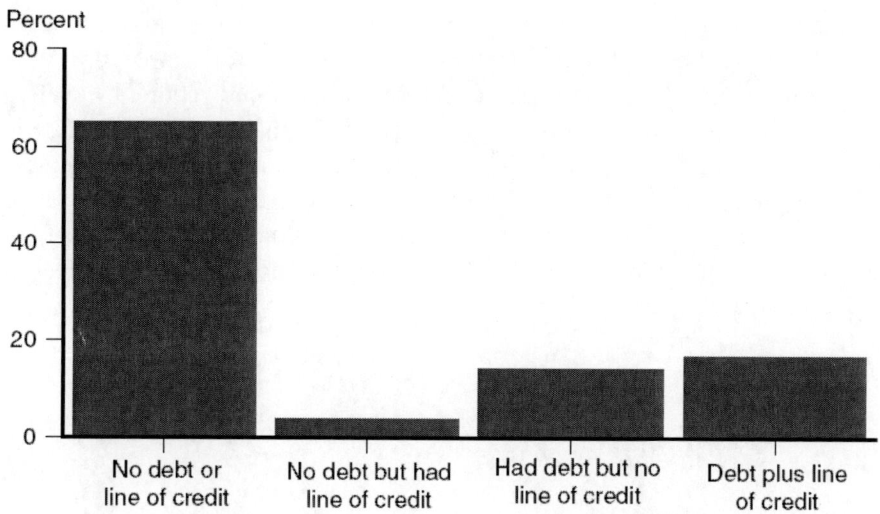

Source: USDA, Agricultural Resource Management Survey.

Figure 36. Farm business use of lines of credit, 2007.

Farms Holding Debt Usually Have Only One Loan from One Lender

Nearly three-fifths of farms that use debt only had one loan from one lender at the end of 2007 (Figure 37). Farms with one loan obtained from a single lender tend to be much smaller, whether measured by acres operated or sales volume, than farms that had multiple loans. Forty-six percent of farms with one loan and one lender had sales less than $10,000 while another 31 percent had sales between $10,000 and $99,999 in 2007. While only about 2 percent of all U.S. farms reported sales over $1,000,000 in 2007, they accounted for 9 percent of farms that had multiple loans and multiple lenders. Even when only one lender is used, large farm operations still more commonly use multiple loans than smaller farms.

Farmers with one lender and multiple loans accounted for 5. 5 percent of farms, but 24 percent of debt reported by all farm operations. The 5. 8 percent of farms with multiple lenders and multiple loans reported 31 percent of all farm-level debt in 2007. The presence of multiple loans and multiple lenders can complicate the relationship between lenders and borrowers, particularly when a farm has multiple operators, because of issues involving collateral and sources of earnings for repayment. These issues are more likely to arise as electronic loan submissions and interactions between borrowers and lenders in different regions become more commonplace. In 2007, for example, operators of $5-million farm businesses that owed debt at year-end reported traveling nearly 3 times as far as all farms, on average, to obtain farm credit, averaging 51 miles in comparison to the 18 miles travelled by smaller farms, on average. Operators of $5-million farm businesses also travelled about twice as far to acquire financing as they did to buy machinery or purchase other inputs, a clear indication that they were willing to go beyond the local credit market to acquire financing (table 3).

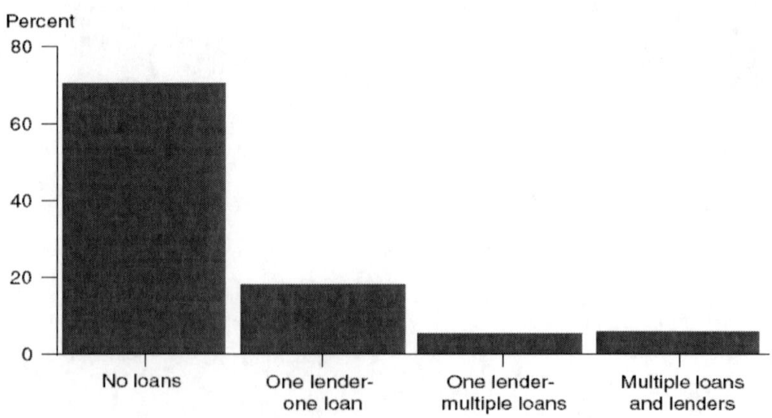

Source: Agricultural Resource Management Survey.

Figure 37. Operators using one or multiple lenders, by percent, 2007.

Table 3. Distances farm businesses traveled to purchase farm inputs in 2007

Annual farm sales							
$9,999	$10,000 – or less	$100,000- $99,999	$500,000 - $499,999	$1,000,000 - $999,999	$5,000,000 $4,999,999	or more	All
Machinery	23.5	26.5	31.7	24.7	27.0	28.0	26.5
Credit	16.8	17.1	19.5	18.3	23.6	51.0	18.1
Other	16.7	16.8	22.1	17.0	20.3	25.8	18.1

Source: 2007 Agricultural Resource Management Survey, USDA, National Agricultural Statistics Service and Economic Research Service.

Farmers Obtain Debt Financing for a Wide Range of Reasons

As a part of the annual ARMS survey, farmers are asked to report the type of loan and primary purpose for their farm-related debt Respondents are first asked to classify loans into one of three broad groups that indicate length of term and likely type of underlying collateral. Namely, farmers are asked if loans are (1) production or other loans for less than 1 year, (2) non-real estate loans for more than 1 year, or (3) real estate loans for more than 1 year. About two-thirds of the outstanding balance on reported farm loans was used to finance real estate purchases (Figure 38). This comes as no surprise since land and buildings make up the largest portion of most farm balance sheets. Non-real estate loans are farm loans that pay for equipment, inputs, or other projects and are expected to take more than a year to repay. Non-real estate loans of more than a year account for 20 percent of farm-level debt reported by farmers. The smallest category of farm loans, in terms of outstanding balance, is production loans, which are used as seasonal infusions of cash to pay for inputs such as feed and fertilizer. Loans of this type account for about 15 percent of farm debt.

Farmers were also asked to report the primary purpose for which they obtained debt financing, regardless of length of term or underlying assets. Response options typically include purchasing real estate (including building or livestock, poultry, or grove development), purchasing feeder livestock, buying other livestock, funding current operating expenses, purchasing machinery and equipment, or consolidating debt. Nearly three-fifths of farmers reported real estate purchases as the primary purpose for borrowing (Figure 39). The next two largest purposes for acquiring farm debt were to pay current operating expenses and to buy machinery and equipment.

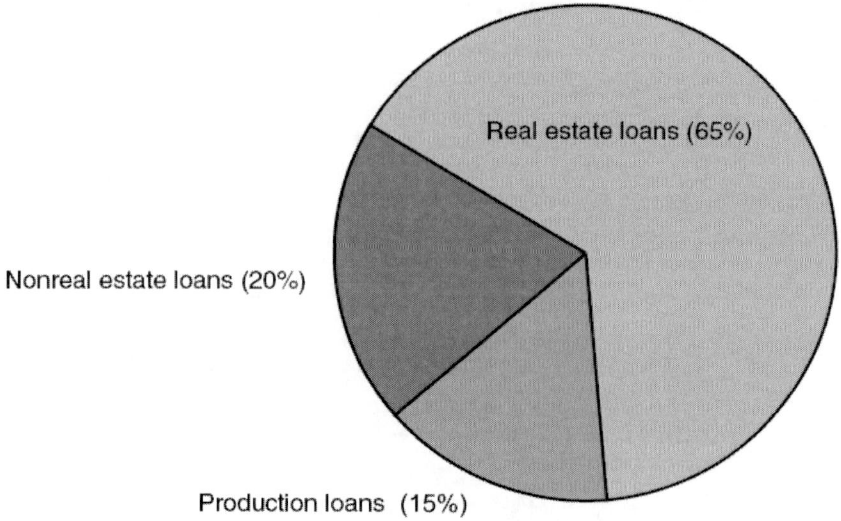

Source: 2007 Agricultural Resource Management Survey, USDA, National Agricultural Statistics Service and Economic Research Service.

Figure 38. Outstanding farm business loans by purpose, 2007.

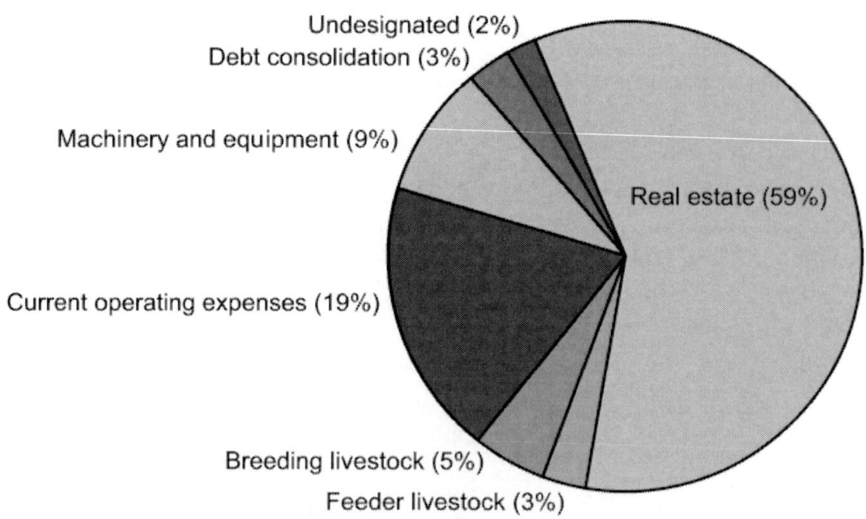

Source: 2007 Agricultural Resource Management Survey, USDA, National Agricultural Statistics Service and Economic Research Service.

Figure 39. Purpose of farm business loan as identified by farm operators, 2007.

Conclusion

Although the future, as always, remains uncertain, agriculture as a whole is relatively safe from a solvency viewpoint. Even though farm debt level has risen in the face of decreasing net farm income, most of the farm sector is well-positioned to weather hard times. However, some farm operators—particularly hog, dairy, and poultry producers—are, on average, more leveraged than other farmers. While these farms are the most highly leveraged, they have also generally been the most profitable. With falling commodity prices shrinking their profit margins, these operations may find themselves at higher risk of financial stress than in past years. This financial stress may manifest itself in a couple different ways.

Mild financial stress may result in farmers having difficulty obtaining loans on favorable terms. In more burdensome cases, farms faced with loan repayment problems may need to negotiate new terms with their lender.

A prolonged period of unusually low commodity prices or high costs would bring about much more severe financial circumstances and structural adjustments.

References

Blocker, A., G. Ibendahl, and J. Anderson. 2003 *Interpreting Farm Financial Ratios*, Extension Circular, Department of Agricultural Economics, Mississippi State University.

Boehlje, Mike, and B. Erickson. 2007. *Adapting Your Management Style, Top Farm Crop Workshop Newsletter*, Department of Agricultural economics, Purdue University, March.

Boyelle, Deborah K., and Fred C. White. 1987. "Factors Affecting Demand and Supply of Agricultural Real Estate Debt," *Western Journal of Agricultural Economics*, 12(2): 174-181.

Brake, John R. 1983. "Financial Crisis in Agriculture: Discussion. " *American Journal of Agricultural Economics*, 65(5): 953-954.

Castle, Emory N., M. H. Becker, and A. G. Nelson. 1972. *Farm Business Management: The Decision-Making Process*, Macmillan Publishing Company, New York.

Duffy, Mike, and Darnell Smith. 2008. *Iowa Land Value Survey.* Iowa State Cooperative Extension, FM 1825, Dec.

Ellinger, Paul. 2009. "Financial Markets and Agricultural Credit at a Time of Uncertainty", *Choices*, 24(1): 32-35.

Hesser, Leon F., and Edward G. Schuh. 1962. "The Demand for Agricultural Mortgage Credit," *Journal of Farm Economics*, 44(5): 1583-1588.

Irwin, George A. 1968. "Three Myths about the Balance Sheet: The Changing Financial Structure of Farming," *American Journal of Agricultural Economics*, 50(5): 1596-1599.

Johnson, James D., and Mitchell Morehart. 1987. "Measurement of Farm Financial Performance: Empirical Issues and Current Status," W. I. Myers Memorial Lecture, Department of Agricultural Economics, Cornell University, Ithaca, NY, Oct.

Johnson, James, M. Morehart., K. Poppe, D. Culver, and C. Salvioni, 2009. "Ownership, Governance, and the Measurement of Income for Farms and Farm Households," Wye City Group Workshop, Rome, Italy, June.

Klinefelter, Danny A., and John B. Penson. 2005. "Growing Complexity of Agricultural Lending Decisions," *Choices*, 20(1): 7-10.

Lins, David. 1972. "Determinants of Net changes in Farm Real Estate Debt," *Agricultural Economic Research*, 24(1): 1-8.

Morehart, Mitch. 2009. "Implications of Macroeconomic Instability for Agriculture Income and Land Values", *Choices* 24(1): 23-31.

Ryan, James T., and Mitchell Morehart. 1992. "Debt Repayment Capacity of Commercial Farm Operators: How Much Debt Can Farmers Afford? *Agricultural Income and Finance*, USDA, ERS, AFO-45, May, pp. 14-22.

U.S. Department of Agriculture, Economic Research Service. 1989. *Major Statistical Series of the U.S. Department of Agriculture, The Balance Sheet*, Agricultural Handbook, No. 671, Vol. 11, May.

U.S. Department of Agriculture, National Agricultural Statistics Service. 1999. *Agricultural Economics and Land Ownership Survey*, Volume 3, Special Studies Part IV (AC97-SP-4)

Williams, Ann N. 1987. "U.S. Farm Non-Real Estate Debt: A Profile and Forecast. " M. S. Thesis, Michigan State University, Department of Agricultural Economics.

APPENDIX: FARM BUSINESS DEBT MEASUREMENT AND DATA SOURCES

Sectorwide estimates of debt are developed as composite measures that use data from multiple sources. Lender types included in the sector-level estimate of debt include commercial banks, life insurance companies, the Farm Credit System, the Farm Service Agency, and a group labeled individuals and others, such as family members. Data for institutional lenders, such as banks, are taken from public sources or are made available by the regulatory agency or lender association. Data from the Farm Service Agency are obtained from administrative sources. The "individuals and others" component of sector level debt estimates is from the Agricultural Resource Management Survey (ARMS). Specific sources for agriculture-related debt as reported by lenders are provided in appendix table 1.

Farm-level estimates of debt are derived directly from farmers' responses to questions included in the annual ARMS survey. At both the farm and sector level, debt represents claims that creditors have on a farm's assets. For farms, as a group, estimates of debt represent the weighted sum of business-level debt as reported by respondents who were interviewed about their farm operation as a part of annual farm business surveys.

ERS publishes a sectorwide balance sheet that pertains only to farm businesses, leaving aside any debt or assets that may used for personal or household circumstances. Historically, ERS also published a balance sheet that included operator households. Both balance sheets, including and excluding operator households, listed similar components. The main difference was that the farm business balance sheet was derived by subtracting the sum of operator dwellings, household equipment, the portion of automobiles and trucks allocated for family use, time deposits and savings bonds, debt on operator dwellings, and the household share of non-real estate debt from the "including" households balance sheet to arrive at an estimate for farm businesses.

Due to data and other limitations, ERS has not developed a sectorwide balance sheet of agriculture that includes household assets and debts since 1992. At the time that ERS discontinued development of a balance sheet that included farm operators' household assets and debt, the complexity of trying to allocate farm household financial accounts between farm and nonfarm activities was a key reason. Moreover, the decision to produce only a farm business-oriented balance sheet recognized that taking into account only the households of primary operators excluded many households, particularly for the largest, most complex farms. Over the last two decades, the financial and organizational structure of farms has become even more complex, with the presence of multiple operators and household participants in farm ownership and governance well documented (Johnson et al., 2009).

Appendix Table 1. Sources of farm sector financial data

Lender	Source
Commercial banks	Federal Reserve System Statistical Release, Agricultural Finance Databook
Farm Credit System	Federal Farm Credit Banks Funding Corporation quarterly Iinformation statement
Farm Service Agency	FSA Farm Loan Program Funding web page
Life insurance companies	ACLI Life Insurers Fact Book—annual update
Individuals and others	Agricultural Resource Management Survey
Commodity Credit Corporation	U.S. Census Bureau Consolidated Federal Funds Report 10.058—Farm Storage Facility Loans

Two adjustments are made to sector-level debt estimates reported by lenders to more accurately reflect debt owed for farm business purposes. The first adjustment reduces the estimate of real estate debt by the share of mortgage debt attributed to operator dwellings. The second adjustment reduces lender-reported debt by the share of farm loans that is used for purposes unrelated to farm business activities (Figure A-1). To ensure balance between asset and debt values, just as debt for dwellings and other nonfarm uses is excluded from the sectorwide estimate of farm business debt, the value of dwellings or the value of any farmer or farm household asset for which debt is secured using farm assets is excluded from the measure of sectorwide assets.

At the farm level, debt represents the claim that creditors have on an individual farm's assets. A key difference between a farm-level and sectorwide balance sheet measurement is that ownership and business boundaries are taken into account at the farm level. This occurs because debt is reported only for the farm as an individual business unit. No estimate of debt owed by landowners or other such persons or entities with which farmers conduct business is included in either the estimate of farm debt or assets. Instead, care is taken to ensure that debt aligns with a farm's reported asset base and with income generated by the farm. The alignment of debt, assets, and income enables current measures of financial performance—e. g., returns and servicing repayment obligations—to be compared among farms and over time.

Where sector-level estimates of debt begin with institutional reports for major lenders such as banks, farm-level estimates are derived from farmers' responses to questions that are included in USDA's Agricultural Resource Management Survey about their farm-based debt use, including questions about debt structure and loan characteristics.

ARMS farm debt questions are developed to first ask respondents whether debt was used in funding the operation of their farms during the previous calendar year, including any seasonal production and other loans taken and repaid during the year.[1] Debt reports include any loans obtained in earlier years, including, for example, loans to buy farmland, to construct buildings or service structures, or to buy equipment. If farmers respond that debt was not used in their businesses in 2007, they were asked why debt, including a line of credit, was not used.[2] If debt use is reported, respondents are then asked if they have an established line of credit and how it was accessed during the calendar year. Again, respondents are provided options: borrowed the full amount of their line of credit, borrowed more by extending the limit, borrowed less, or did not borrow against their line. This line of questioning is followed by questions centered on the use of seasonal production loans that were taken and repaid during the calendar year, and by a series of questions to obtain information about the characteristics of the largest four or five loans outstanding on December 31 of the calendar year. To round out a complete accounting for debt owed, respondents are asked about any other debt in excess of that accounted for by the largest loan sources.

Respondents are not only asked about the amount owed and lenders from whom a loan was obtained, but also about the terms of each of their largest loans. For example, questions are asked about date of origin, and the term and interest rate associated with loans, along with questions about loan purpose and type, and whether rates are fixed or adjustable. If respondents indicate that they have loans with an adjustable rate, they are also asked how often the loan is repriced. Responses to the loan volume, structure, and pricing questions are used in conjunction with estimates of income to develop an indication of debt service capability and to assess how use of debt service capacity varies among farms and over time.

Sector-level debt, as developed from lender reports, includes all debt secured by farm real estate or other assets. This is why an estimate of debt used either for nonfarm purposes or associated with operator dwellings has to be subtracted to arrive at an estimate of farm business debt for the sector. At the farm level, respondents are asked directly to exclude debt used for nonfarm purposes even if the loan is secured by a farm operation's assets. Instead, "off-farm" debt secured by farm assets is recorded along with debt obtained using any other source of collateral to construct a balance sheet for the households of farm operators.

Following these procedures enables ERS estimates of household-based assets and debts to be assessed apart from assets and debt of farms as business operations. Repayment capabilities of farm households may then be measured based on both farm and nonfarm sources of debt and income. Meanwhile, farm business estimates draw only on farm-based debt and income.

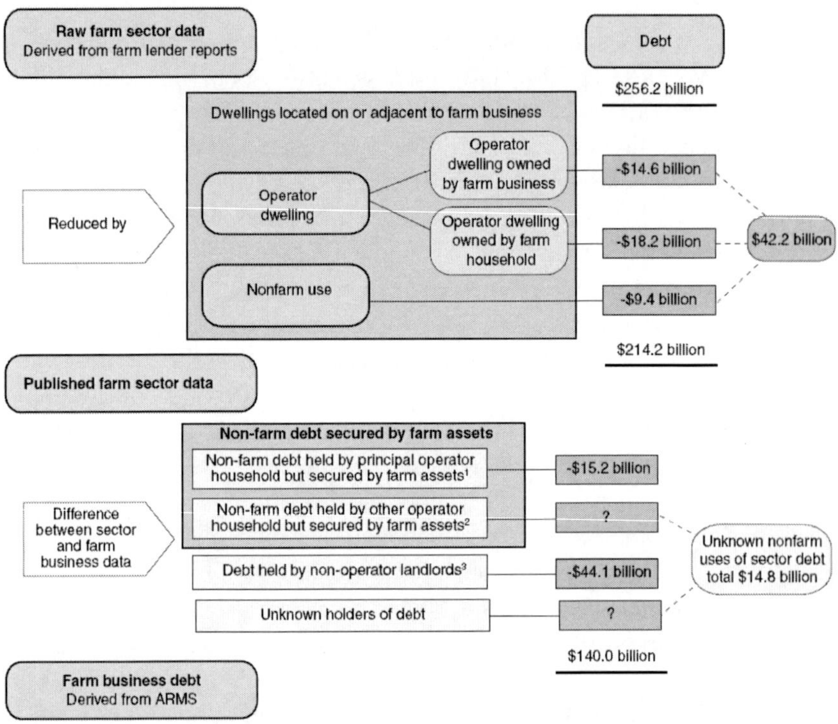

[1]ARMS estimates that 6.42% of U.S. farm sector debt is used by households for nonfarm purposes but is secured by farm business assets.

[2]Estimated using average amount of household debt secured by farm assets.

[3]1999 USDA Agricultural Economics and Land Ownership (AELOS) survey estimates that 17.2% of real estate debt is held by non-operator landlords.

Figure A-1. Relationship between estimates of debt reported by level of aggregation, 2007.

Sectorwide and farm-level estimates of debt do not show the same magnitude of debt use within the farm sector (Figure A1). This is expected since farm-level debt reported for farms as individual businesses is a subset of total sector-level debt. This occurs for two reasons. First, farmers report use of farm-based debt for non-business purposes and for the purchase of dwellings. Second, owners and operators of farm businesses are only a subset of all borrowers of loan funds that are either secured by farm assets or are associated with an agricultural activity (Irwin, 1968). For example, the most recent Agricultural Economics and Land Ownership Survey (AELOS), conducted in 1999, showed that landlords held 17.2 percent of the total amount of debt reported by operators and landlords together.[3] The AELOS revealed nonoperator owners to be active participants in farm real estate markets, with non-operators accounting for nearly 30 percent of the number of individuals acquiring land in 1999 and 19 percent of the purchasers who acquired owner financing.

AELOS tracked time periods, by 10-year increments, when owners reported acquiring land. Based on responses to these questions, nonoperator owners have remained an integral part of farmland markets over time, ranging from 32 to 35 percent of purchasers during the 1973-98 timeframe. Recent data from Iowa show that nonoperator landlords continued to be active participants in farmland markets. In 2007, 49 percent of farmland owners did not live on owned farmland, with 40 percent of farmland owned by persons who did not farm. Of Iowa farmland owned by nonoperators, 13 percent was financed by mortgage and 1 percent was under contract (Duffy and Smith, 2008).

Farm-level estimates derived from the annual ARMS survey provide the only measure of farm debt that is detailed enough to examine the distribution of debt among farms in conjunction with income earned by farms that hold debt financing. Moreover, ARMS is the only national-level farm source of farm debt, conducted on an ongoing basis, sufficient to provide a foundation from which to examine changes in debt use and concentration among farms and over time.

The only other data source able to provide any perspective about the distribution of debt among farms is the Census of Agriculture, and even this meager glimpse of debt use is indirect. Census does not ask farmers directly about use of debt in their businesses. Comparing the share of farms with interest expenses from the Census of Agriculture with the share of farms that report debt in ARMS reveals a similar trend.

Both data sources show share of farms reporting debt declining dramatically from the mid-1980s. through 2007 (Figure A-2). Census data on interest expenses may imply the level of debt owed by farmers. We used interest rates derived from the ARMS for both real estate and non-real estate debt to impute debt.

This was done by assuming that real estate was in year two of a 7-year loan. Since the census is reported in thousands of dollars, the debt service for repaying $1,000 was determined. Interest charges were summed for the year and used to impute an implied debt estimate from census interest expense. Once again, trends are similar, showing a growing amount of debt reported by farms. Obviously, changing the assumption embedded in Figure A-3 would alter the amount of debt implied by the census. Still, the main idea drawn from Figure A-1—that farm business debt does not account for all debt labeled as farm debt—would remain largely intact.

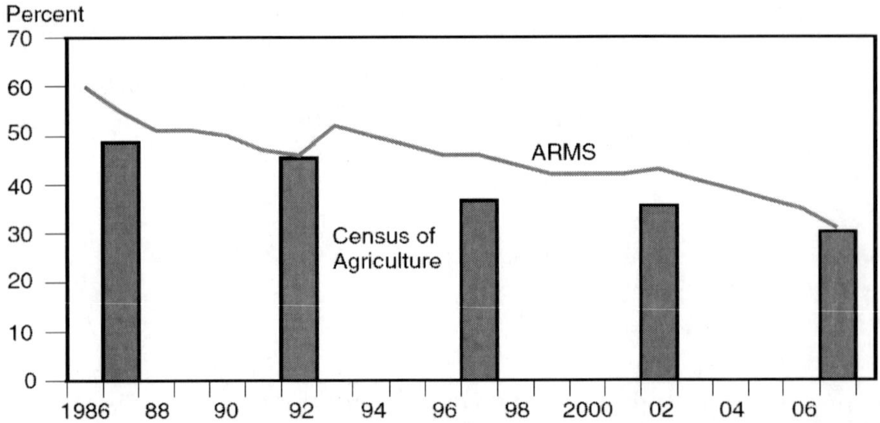

Note: Farms were determined to be debt holders in the Census of Agriculture if they reported interest expenses.

Source: Agricultural Resource Management Survey and Farm Costs and Returns Survey, USDA, National Agricultural Statistics Service and Economic Research Service; and the Census of Agriculture, USDA, National Agricultural Statistics Service.

Figure A-2. Share of farms reporting debt from the Census of Agriculture and ARMS, 1986-2007.

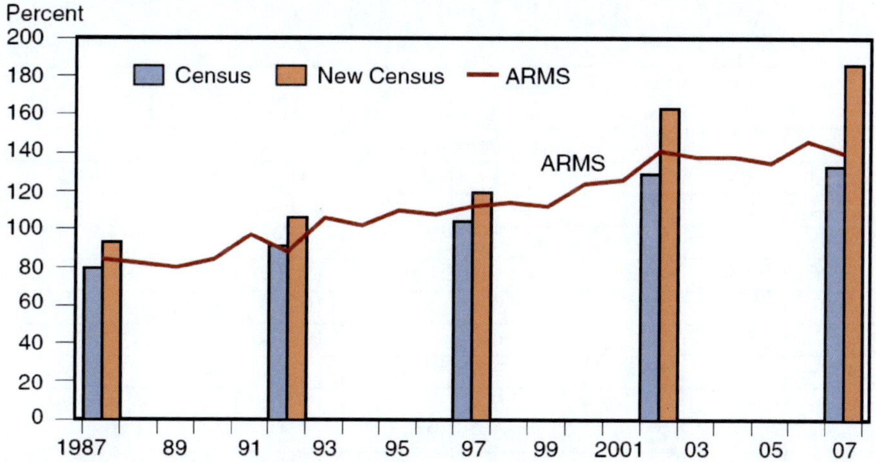

Note: Prior to 1996, farm-level surveys were labeled as Farm Costs and Return Surveys. Census instructs respondents to include interest on such items as feed, seed, fertilizer, so it is not clear whether this would include accounts payable. ARMS loans outstanding and estimates of accounts payable and accrued interest are included to enable comparison.

Source: Agricultural Resource Management Survey and Farm Costs and Returns Survey, USDA, National Agricultural Statistics Service and Economic Research Service; and the Census of Agriculture, USDA, National Agricultural Statistics Service.

Figure A-3. Comparing Census of Agriculture implied debt to farm business debt, 1987-2007.

Appendix Table 2. Farm sector financial statistics, 1984-2009f

	Real estate	Nonreal estate	Total debt	Equity	Assets	Net cash income	DRCU
			$ billion				
1984	101.4	87.4	188.8	709.0	897.8	36.0	93%
1985	94.1	78.1	172.1	603.8	775.9	45.6	72%
1986	84.1	67.2	151.3	570.7	722.0	46.5	62%
1987	75.8	62.7	138.5	618.0	756.5	52.6	51%
1988	70.8	62.3	133.1	655.4	788.5	53.7	49%
1989	68.8	62.3	131.0	682.7	813.7	53.5	51%
1990	67.6	63.5	131.1	709.5	840.6	53.8	49%
1991	67.5	64.4	131.9	712.3	844.2	51.4	50%
1992	67.9	63.7	131.6	736.2	867.8	56.9	43%

Appendix Table 2. (Continued)

	Real estate	Nonreal estate	Total debt	Equity	Assets	Net cash income	DRCU
			$ billion				
1993	68.4	65.9	134.3	774.9	909.2	60.8	41%
1994	69.9	69.0	138.9	795.8	934.8	53.7	47%
1995	71.7	71.3	143.0	822.8	965.8	54.5	51%
1996	74.4	74.2	148.6	854.3	1002.9	60.9	46%
1997	78.5	78.4	156.9	894.4	1051.3	60.9	50%
1998	83.1	81.5	164.6	918.8	1083.4	57.7	54%
1999	87.2	80.5	167.7	971.1	1138.8	57.9	54%
2000	84.7	79.2	163.9	1039.3	1203.2	57.3	55%
2001	88.5	82.1	170.7	1085.3	1255.9	62.1	51%
2002	95.4	81.8	177.2	1126.8	1304.0	51.3	58%
2003	94.1	81.0	175.1	1203.6	1378.8	71.5	44%
2004	96.9	86.1	183.0	1434.6	1617.6	82.3	40%
2005	104.8	91.6	196.4	1583.0	1779.4	86.8	47%
2006	108.1	94.9	196.4	1851.0	2047.4	68.8	60%
2007	112.7	101.4	214.1	1841.2	2055.5	78.2	57%
2008	130.7	109.4	240.1	1765.5	2005.5	97.5	48%
2009	130.7	103.4	234.1	1701.5	1935.6	68.2	63%

Source: USDA, Economic Research Service.

Appendix Table 3. USDA Agricultural Resource Management Survey estimates, by debt classification, 2007

	Debt classification		
Item	No lender debt payable	Debt payable to lender(s)	48-State total
Number of farms	1,510,418	686,348	2,196,766
Percent of farms	68.8	31.2	100.0
Value of production ($1,000)	96,068,345	194,145,460	290,213,805
Percent of value of production	33.1	66.9	100.0
		Acres per farm	
Land operated per farm	290	684	413
Total farm loan debt	0	138,574,596	138,574,596

Item	Debt classification		48-State total
	No lender debt payable	Debt payable to lender(s)	
Percent of debt held	0.0	100.0	100.0
Farm operation income statement:		*Dollars per farm*	
Gross cash income	64,262	242,839	120,056
Less: **Cash expenses**	48,639	192,295	93,522
Variable	40,685	151,309	75,248
Fixed	7,954	40,985	18,274
Equals: **Net cash farm income**	15,623	50,544	26,533
Balance sheet characteristics:		*$1,000*	
Value of total farm financial assets	1,066,076,481	813,836,838	1,879,913,319
Total farm financial debt*	2,049,521	146,145,643	148,195,164
Accounts payable	2,049,521	3,413,749	5,463,270
Seasonal loans taken and repaid during year	9,656,030	32,054,512	41,710,543
		Percent	
Seasonal loans taken and repaid during year	23.2	76.8	100.0
Profitability:		*Percent*	
Return on assets	0.27	3.49	1.67
Operating profit margin	2.56	15.05	10.41
Debt distributions:			
Sales classes:			
$9,999 or less	68.1	36.7	58.3
$10,000-$99,999	23.5	28.8	25.1
$100,000-$499,999	6.4	21.7	11.2
$500,000-$999,999	1.2	7.8	3.3
$1,000,000-$4,999,999	0.7	4.6	1.9
$5,000,000 or more	0.1	0.5	0.2
Farm types			

Appendix Table 3. (Continued)

	Debt classification		
Item	No lender debt payable	Debt payable to lender(s)	48-State total
Cash grain and soybean	10.7	21.9	14.2
Other field crops	24.6	14.5	21.5
High-value crops	6.4	6.3	6.3
Beef cattle	31.0	28.5	30.2
Hogs	0.9	2.6	1.5
Poultry	0.8	3.9	1.8
Dairy	1.4	6.3	2.9
General livestock	24.2	16.0	21.6
Tenure:			
Full owner	72.9	47.5	64.9
Part owner	21.2	44.7	28.6
Tenant	5.9	7.8	6.5
Operator age:			
Less than 35 years	3.9	8.1	5.2
35 to 44	9.7	18.3	12.4
45 to 54	21.0	30.2	23.9
55 to 64 years	31.3	29.4	30.7
65 years or older	34.1	13.9	27.8
Mileage to obtain inputs:		*Miles*	
Miles to buy machinery	22.3	26.5	23.7
Miles to obtain credit	14.2	18.1	16.0
Miles to do farm related business/purchasing	16.2	18.1	16.8

* Total farm financial debt = total farm loan debt + total accounts payable + total accrued interest. Based on 6,614 observations (6,179 households, 435 non-households). Version=1 only. Source: 2007 USDA Agricultural Resource Management Survey.

Appendix Table 4. USDA Agricultural Resource Management Survey estimates, by number of lenders and loans, 2007

Item		Debt classification			
	No loans	One lender One loan	One lender with multiple loans	Multiple lenders and loans	48-State tota
Number of farms	1,548,993	399,198	120,148	128,427	2,196,766
Percent of farms	70.5	18.2	5.5	5.8	100.0
Value of production ($1,000)	114,312,095	76,912,750	44,791,775	54,197,185	290,213,805
Percent of value of production	39.4	26.5	15.4	18.7	100.0
			Acres per farm		
Land operated per farm	317	500	695	1,035	413
		$1,000			
Total farm loan debt	15,370,791	46,986,186	33,680,175	42,537,444	138,574,596
Percent of debt held	11.1	33.9	24.3	30.7	100.0
Farm operation income statement:			*Dollars per farm*		
Gross cash income	72,479	154,750	325,290	394,049	120,056
Less: Cash expenses	55,102	128,165	250,187	302,676	93,522
Variable	45,680	102,327	196,703	234,084	75,248
Fixed	9,422	25,838	53,484	68,592	18,274
Equals: Net cash farm income	17,377	26,585	75,103	91,373	26,533
Balance sheet characteristics:			*$1,000*		
Value of total farm financial assets	1,134,208,467	371,974,302	164,491,753	209,238,797	1,879,913,319
Total farm financial debt	18,203,612	49,576,858	35,469,958	44,944,736	148,195,164
Accounts payable	2,371,704	1,181,059	779,365	1,131,142	5,463,270

Appendix Table 4. (Continued)

Item		Debt classification			
	No loans	One lender One loan	One lender with multiple loans	Multiple lenders and loans	48-State tota
Seasonal loans taken & repaid during year	10,085,145	11,410,366	8,175,196	12,039,836	41,710,543
			Percent		
Seasonal loans taken & repaid during year	24.2	27.4	19.6	28.9	100.0
Profitability:					
Return on assets (percent)	0.53	1.80	4.50	5.37	1.67
Operating profit margin (percent)	4.65	9.49	17.18	19.15	10.41
Debt distributions:					
Sales class:					
$9,999 or less	67.1	45.8	29.2	17.7	58.3
$10,000-$99,999	23.5	30.9	26.9	24.4	25.1
$100,000-$499,999	6.8	15.9	27.2	34.1	11.2
$500,000-$999,999	1.6	4.5	9.3	14.8	3.3
$1,000,000-$4,999,999	0.9	2.5	6.7	8.4	1.9
$5,000,000 or more	0.1	0.3	0.7	0.6	0.2
Farm type:					
Cash grain and soybean	11.0	17.2	27.1	31.0	14.2
Other field crops	24.4	14.8	15.7	11.5	21.5
High-value crops	6.5	6.3	6.3	4.9	6.3

Item		Debt classification			
	No loans	One lender One loan	One lender with multiple loans	Multiple lenders and loans	48-State tota
Beef cattle	30.7	31.1	28.8	23.0	30.2
Hogs	0.9	2.9	1.3	3.4	1.5
Poultry	0.9	3.8	4.3	3.6	1.8
Dairy	1.5	4.6	7.4	11.2	2.9
General livestock	24.1	19.2	9.0	11.3	21.6
Tenure:					
Full owner	72.4	54.7	38.4	31.4	64.9
Part owner	21.7	36.9	52.9	62.2	28.6
Tenant	5.9	8.4	8.7	6.5	6.5
Operator age:					
Less than 35 years	3.9	8.2	8.3	8.9	5.2
35 to 44	9.7	17.3	23.6	18.8	12.4
45 to 54	21.3	30.6	25.9	32.4	23.9
55 to 64 years	31.6	27.0	32.5	29.9	30.7
65 years or older	33.5	16.9	9.7	10.1	27.8
Mileage to obtain inputs:			*Miles*		
Miles to buy machinery	22.4	25.5	25.8	29.7	23.7
Miles to obtain credit	14.3	18.4	17.1	19.0	16.0
Miles to do farm related business/purchasing	16.4	17.5	18.0	18.4	16.8

** Total farm financial debt = total farm loan debt + total accounts payable + total accrued interest.

Based on 6,614 observations (6,179 households, 435 non-households). Expansion factor was VER1WT0. Version=1 only. Source: 2007 USDA Agricultural Resource Management Survey.

Appendix Table 5. Farm financial, operator, and structural characteristics for farm operations with debt grouped by sales class, 2007

		Debt classification					
Item	Operation has debt payable and gross sales of $9,999 or less	Operation has debt payable and gross sales of $10,000-$99,999	Operation has debt payable and gross sales of $100,000-$499,999	Operation has debt payable and gross sales of $500,000-$999,999	Operation has debt payable and gross sales of $1,000,000-$4,999,999	Operation has debt payable and gross sales of $5,000,000 or more	48-State total
Number of farms	251,800	197,330	148,955	53,548	31,231	3,483	686,348
Percent of farms	36.7	28.8	21.7	7.8	4.6	0.5	100.0
Value of production ($1,000)	1,041,360	8,707,882	41,449,251	38,459,682	61,165,207	43,322,078	194,145,460
Percent of value of production	0.5	4.5	21.3	19.8	31.5	22.3	100.0
		Acres per farm					
Land operated per farm	87	436	1,238	1,601	2,607	2,909	684
Total farm loan debt	23,973,914	19,891,992	31,233,366	23,028,490	25,790,824	14,656,011	138,574,596
Share of debt held	17.3	14.4	22.5	16.6	18.6	10.6	100.0

		Debt classification					
Item	Operation has debt payable and gross sales of $9,999 or less	Operation has debt payable and gross sales of $10,000-$99,999	Operation has debt payable and gross sales of $100,000-$499,999	Operation has debt payable and gross sales of $500,000-$999,999	Operation has debt payable and gross sales of $1,000,000-$4,999,999	Operation has debt payable and gross sales of $5,000,000 or more	48-State total
Farm operation income statement;		*Dollars per farm*					
Gross cash income	6,178	47,556	244,283	618,268	1,652,012	9,945,999	242,839
Less: Cash expenses	19,771	52,969	193,668	452,077	1,220,483	7,285,768	192,295
Variable	10,080	37,291	145,789	344,321	995,248	6,522,122	151,309
Fixed	9,690	15,678	47,880	107,756	225,235	763,646	40,985
Equals: Net cash farm income	-13,592	-5,412	50,614	166,191	431,529	2,660,231	50,544
Balance sheet characteristics;		*$ 1,000*					
Value of total farm financial assets	125,684,885	160,792,622	222,914,359	129,397,490	130,995,674	44,051,809	813,836,838
Total farm financial debt*	24,840,908	20,771,069	33,063,271	24,517,850	27,502,022	15,450,523	146,145,643
Accounts payable	147,756	282,298	892,890	798,501	937,471	354,832	3,413,749
Seasonal loans taken and repaid during year	305,264	1,814,195	8,684,523	8,399,013	9,690,139	3,161,379	32,054,512
		Percent					
Seasonal loans taken and repaid during year	1.0	5.7	27.1	26.2	30.2	9.9	100.0

Appendix Table 5. (Continued)

		Debt classification					
Item	Operation has debt payable and gross sales of $9,999 or less	Operation has debt payable and gross sales of $10,000-$99,999	Operation has debt payable and gross sales of $100,000-$499,999	Operation has debt payable and gross sales of $500,000-$999,999	Operation has debt payable and gross sales of $1,000,000-$4,999,999	Operation has debt payable and gross sales of $5,000,000 or more	48-State total
Profitability;							
Return on assets (*percent*)	-2.50	-2.88	2.06	7.13	10.25	20.36	3.49
Operating profit margin (*percent*) -	66.01	-38.68	10.76	24.11	24.03	25.24	15.05
Debt distributions: Sales class:				*Percent*			
$9,999 or less	100.0	0.0	0.0	0.0	0.0	0.0	36.7
$10,000-$99,999	0.0	100.0	0.0	0.0	0.0	0.0	28.8
$100,000-$499,999	0.0	0.0	100.0	0.0	0.0	0.0	21.7
$500,000-$999,999	0.0	0.0	0.0	100.0	0.0	0.0	7.8
$1,000,000-$4,999,999	0.0	0.0	0.0	0.0	100.0	0.0	4.6
$5,000,000 or more	0.0	0.0	0.0	0.0	0.0	100.0	0.5
Farm type:							

	Debt classification						
Item	Operation has debt payable and gross sales of $9,999 or less	Operation has debt payable and gross sales of $10,000-$99,999	Operation has debt payable and gross sales of $100,000-$499,999	Operation has debt payable and gross sales of $500,000-$999,999	Operation has debt payable and gross sales of $1,000,000-$4,999,999	Operation has debt payable and gross sales of $5,000,000 or more	48-State total
Cash grain and soybean	2.9	20.9	46.6	45.5	24.3	5.0	21.9
Other field crops	23.5	13.6	4.8	7.7	8.1	0.6	14.5
High value crops	2.9	9.1	6.5	7.8	10.5	21.0	6.3
Beef cattle	29.5	45.1	15.5	10.4	8.5	28.6	28.5
Hogs	2.5	1.1	1.8	4.6	12.2	9.1	2.6
Poultry	1.8	0.3	5.2	14.5	18.3	8.1	3.9
Dairy	0.0	4.3	16.8	8.5	14.4	25.2	6.3
General livestock	36.9	5.6	2.7	1.0	3.7	2.4	16.0
Tenure:							
Full owner	75.2	43.9	20.4	20.0	24.6	37.9	47.5
Part owner	21.7	48.9	65.7	71.4	59.4	40.3	44.7
Tenant	3.1	7.2	13.9	8.6	16.1	21.8	7.8
Operator age:							
Less than 35 years	7.2	8.2	9.7	8.3	7.5	8.9	8.1
35 to 44	19.8	16.9	17.9	16.6	20.7	17.8	18.3
45 to 54	31.7	24.8	31.5	34.9	36.3	33.2	30.2
55 to 64 years	28.5	31.3	29.0	30.3	26.2	29.0	29.4

Appendix Table 5. (Continued)

		Debt classification					
Item	Operation has debt payable and gross sales of $9,999 or less	Operation has debt payable and gross sales of $10,000-$99,999	Operation has debt payable and gross sales of $100,000-$499,999	Operation has debt payable and gross sales of $500,000-$999,999	Operation has debt payable and gross sales of $1,000,000-$4,999,999	Operation has debt payable and gross sales of $5,000,000 or more	48-State total
65 years or older	12.9	18.7	11.9	9.9	9.2	11.0	13.9
Mileage to obtain inputs:				*Miles*			
Miles to buy machinery	23.5	26.5	31.7	24.7	27.0	28.0	26.5
Miles to obtain credit	16.8	17.1	19.5	18.3	23.6	51.0	18.1
Miles to do farm-related business/purchasing	16.7	16.8	22.1	17.0	20.3	25.8	18.1

* Total farm financial debt = total farm loan debt + total accounts payable + total accrued interest.

Based on 6,614 observations (6,179 households, 435 non-households). Expansion factor was VER1WT0. Version=1 only. Source: 2007 USDA Agricultural Resource Management Survey.

Appendix Table 6. Farm financial, operator, and structural characteristics for farm operations by debt classification and line of credit, 2007

	Debt Classification				
Item	No debt and no line of credit established	No debt but had an established line of credit in 2006	Operation had debt in 2006 but no established line of credit	Operation had debt in 2006 plus an established line of credit	48-State total
Number of farms	1,428,027	82,391	312,415	373,933	2,196,766
Percent of farms	65.0	3.8	14.2	17.0	100.0
Value of production ($1,000)	66,341,733	29,726,612	38,462,516	155,682,944	290,213,805
Percent of value of production	22.9	10.2	13.3	53.6	100.0
			Acres per farm		
Land operated per farm	258	846	345	968	413
Total farm loan debt	0	0	41,067,448	97,507,148	138,574,596
Percent of debt held	0.0	0.0	29.6	70.4	100.0
Farm operation income statement:			*Dollars per farm*		
Gross cash income	46,243	376,564	87,601	372,538	120,056
Less: **Cash expenses**	35,995	267,797	76,323	289,187	93,522
Variable	30,299	220,701	57,821	229,417	75,248
Fixed	5,696	47,096	18,502	59,770	18,274
Equals: **Net cash farm income**	10,249	108,767	11,278	83,351	26,533
Balance sheet characteristics:			*$1,000*		
Value of total farm financial assets	951,274,058	114,802,423	247,722,543	566,114,295	1,879,913,319

Appendix Table 6. (Continued)

		Debt Classification			
Item	No debt and no line of credit established	No debt but had an established line of credit in 2006	Operation had debt in 2006 but no established line of credit	Operation had debt in 2006 plus an established line of credit	48-State total
Total farm financial debt*	1,447,436	602,085	42,874,041	103,271,602	148,195,164
Accounts payable	1,447,436	602,085	574,543	2,839,206	5,463,270
Seasonal loans taken and repaid during year	449,322	9,206,709	1,031,434	31,023,078	41,710,543
			Percent		
Seasonal loans taken and repaid during year	1.1	22.1	2.5	74.4	100.0
Profitability:					
Return on assets (*percent*)	-0.41	5.85	0.18	4.95	1.67
Operating profit margin (*percent*)	-4.92	20.21	1.36	17.89	10.41
Debt distributions: Sales class:					
$9,999 or less	71.2	13.9	54.9	21.5	58.3
$10,000-$99,999	22.7	36.6	27.8	29.5	25.1
$100,000-$499,999	4.9	31.7	12.6	29.3	11.2
$500,000-$999,999	0.7	10.9	2.7	12.1	3.3
$1,000,000-$4,999,999	0.4	6.2	1.9	6.8	1.9
$5,000,000 or more	0.1	0.6	0.1	0.8	0.2

Item	Debt Classification				48-State total
	No debt and no line of credit established	No debt but had an established line of credit in 2006	Operation had debt in 2006 but no established line of credit	Operation had debt in 2006 plus an established line of credit	
Farm type:					
Cash grain and soybean	8.3	52.1	10.1	31.7	14.2
Other field crops	25.3	12.8	19.9	10.0	21.5
High-value crops	6.2	8.8	7.3	5.4	6.3
Beef cattle	31.8	18.0	28.3	28.7	30.2
Hogs	0.9	0.8	2.6	2.7	1.5
Poultry	0.8	0.7	4.9	3.1	1.8
Dairy	1.4	2.1	4.7	7.7	2.9
General livestock	25.3	4.7	22.2	10.8	21.6
Tenure:					
Full owner	74.8	38.6	63.9	33.8	64.9
Part owner	20.1	40.3	31.1	56.2	28.6
Tenant	5.1	21.0	5.0	10.1	6.5
Operator age:					
Less than 35 years	3.7	6.9	6.7	9.4	5.2
35 to 44	9.5	13.5	19.9	17.0	12.4
45 to 54	20.9	23.3	30.6	29.8	23.9
55 to 64 years	31.2	33.5	28.9	29.9	30.7
65 years or older	34.7	22.9	14.0	13.9	27.8

Appendix Table 6. (Continued)

Item	Debt Classification				48-State total
	No debt and no line of credit established	No debt but had an established line of credit in 2006	Operation had debt in 2006 but no established line of credit	Operation had debt in 2006 plus an established line of credit	
Mileage to obtain inputs:			*Miles*		
Miles to buy machinery	21.8	29.4	25.7	27.1	23.7
Miles to obtain credit	13.7	18.7	16.8	19.2	16.0
Miles to do farm-related purchasing	16.2	15.9	17.5	18.7	16.8

* Total farm financial debt = total farm loan debt + total accounts payable + total accrued interest.

Based on 6,614 observations (6,179 households, 435 non-households). Expansion factor was VER1WT0. Version=1 only. Source: 2007 USDA Agricultural Resource Management Survey.

Appendix Table 7. Farm financial, operator, and structural characteristics for farm operations by debt classification, 2007

Item	Debt classification No lender debt payable	Debt payable to lender(s)	48-State total
Number of farms	1,510,418	686,348	2,196,766
Percent of farms	68.8	31.2	100.0
Value of production ($1,000)	96,068,345	194,145,460	290,213,805
Percent of value of production	33.1	66.9	100.0
		Acres per farm	
Land operated per farm	290	684	413
Total farm loan debt	0	138,574,596	138,574,596
Percent of debt held	0.0	100.0	100.0
Farm operation income statement:		*Dollars per farm*	
Gross cash income	64,262	242,839	120,056
Less: **Cash expenses**	48,639	192,295	93,522
Variable	40,685	151,309	75,248
Fixed	7,954	40,985	18,274
Equals: **Net cash farm income**	15,623	50,544	26,533
Balance sheet characteristics:		*$1,000*	
Value of total farm financial assets	1,066,076,481	813,836,838	1,879,913,319
Total farm financial debt*	2,049,521	146,145,643	148,195,164
Accounts payable	2,049,521	3,413,749	5,463,270
Seasonal loans taken and repaid during year	9,656,030	32,054,512	41,710,543
		Percent	

Appendix Table 7. (Continued)

Item	Debt classification		48-State total
	No lender debt payable	Debt payable to lender(s)	
Seasonal loans taken and repaid during year	23.2	76.8	100.0
Profitability:			
Return on assets (percent)	0.27	3.49	1.67
Operating profit margin (percent)	2.56	15.05	10.41
Debt distributions:			
Sales class $9,999 or less	68.1	36.7	58.3
$10,000-$99,999	23.5	28.8	25.1
$100,000-$499,999	6.4	21.7	11.2
$500,000-$999,999	1.2	7.8	3.3
$1,000,000-$4,999,999	0.7	4.6	1.9
$5,000,000 or more	0.1	0.5	0.2
Farm type:	*Percent*		
Cash grain and soybean	10.7	21.9	14.2
Other field crops	24.6	14.5	21.5
High-value crops	6.4	6.3	6.3
Beef cattle	31.0	28.5	30.2
Hogs	0.9	2.6	1.5
Poultry	0.8	3.9	1.8
Dairy	1.4	6.3	2.9
General livestock	24.2	16.0	21.6
Tenure:			

Item	Debt classification		48-State total
	No lender debt payable	Debt payable to lender(s)	
Full owner	72.9	47.5	64.9
Part owner	21.2	44.7	28.6
Tenant	5.9	7.8	6.5
Operator age:			
Less than 35 years	3.9	8.1	5.2
35 to 44	9.7	18.3	12.4
45 to 54	21.0	30.2	23.9
55 to 64 years	31.3	29.4	30.7
65 years or older	34.1	13.9	27.8
Mileage to obtain inputs:		*Miles*	
Miles to buy machinery	22.3	26.5	23.7
Miles to obtain credit	14.2	18.1	16.0
Miles to do farm-related business/purchasing	16.2	18.1	16.8

* Total farm financial debt = total farm loan debt + total accounts payable + total accrued interest.

Based on 6,614 observations (6,179 households, 435 non-households). Expansion factor was VER1WT0. Version=1 only. Source: 2007 USDA Agricultural Resource Management Survey.

Appendix Table 8. Farm financial, operator, and structural characteristics for farm operations by debt-to-asset-ratio groupings, 2007

		Debt-to-asset ratio					
Item	No debt	.01 -. 10	.11 -. 40	.41 -. 70	.71 - 1.0	Over 1.0	48-State total
Number of farms	1,510,418	262,079	299,274	93,653	20,993	10,349	2,196,766
Percent of farms	68.8	11.9	13.6	4.3	1.0	0.5	100.0
Value of production ($1,000)	96,068,345	54,708,183	94,924,662	30,145,921	8,657,475	5,709,218	290,213,805
Percent of value of production	33.1	18.9	32.7	10.4	3.0	2.0	100.0
	Acres per farm						
Land operated per farm	290	764	724	383	512	597	413
Total farm loan debt	0	15,029,493	72,947,350	33,314,305	9,707,735	7,575,713	138,574,596
Percent of debt held	0.0	10.8	52.6	24.0	7.0	5.5	100.0
Farm operation income statement:	*Dollars per farm*						
Gross cash income	64,262	184,626	281,895	252,293	328,058	329,182	120,056
Less: **Cash expenses**	48,639	146,749	218,849	206,358	271,385	290,104	93,522
Variable	40,685	118,573	170,990	161,478	208,826	202,505	75,248
Fixed	7,954	28,176	47,858	44,880	62,559	87,599	18,274
Equals: Net cash farm income	15,623	37,877	63,046	45,935	a56,673	a39,078	26,533
Balance sheet characteristics:				*$ 1,000*			
Value of total farm financial assets	1,066,076,481	376,301,883	354,416,446	65,848,767	12,358,386	4,911,356	1,879,913,319
Total farm financial debt*	2,049,521	16,537,265	76,849,574	34,705,558	10,153,447	7,899,800	148,195,164
Accounts payable	2,049,521	1,056,858	1,713,781	391,814	154,481	96,815	5,463,270

		Debt-to-asset ratio					
Item	No debt	.01 -. 10	.11 -. 40	.41 -. 70	.71 - 1.0	Over 1.0	48-State total
Seasonal loans taken and repaid during year	9,656,030	7,617,572	18,613,340	4,414,537	872,203	536,861	41,710,543
Percent							
Seasonal loans taken and repaid during year	23.2	18.3	44.6	10.6	2.1	1.3	100.0
Profitability:				*Percent*			
Return on assets	0.27	1.66	4.83	5.46	7.26	11.93	1.67
Operating profit margin	2.56	11.09	17.81	13.93	12.53	16.47	10.41
Debt distributions:							
Sales class:							
$9,999 or less	68.1	32.7	34.0	50.2	48.2	69.9	58.3
$10,000-$99,999	23.5	37.1	25.3	21.2	19.6	4.6	25.1
$100,000-$499,999	6.4	20.0	25.9	15.1	20.3	7.3	11.2
$500,000-$999,999	1.2	6.8	8.9	7.2	6.3	10.7	3.3
$1,000,000-$4,999,999	0.7	3.2	5.4	5.5	4.3	5.5	1.9
$5,000,000 or more	0.1	0.2	0.6	0.8	1.3	2.1	0.2
Farm type:				*Percent*			
Cash grain and soybean	10.7	22.7	24.1	15.6	14.0	7.7	14.2
Other field crops	24.6	16.1	12.4	16.3	20.8	8.7	21.5
High-value crops	6.4	6.0	6.3	5.9	2.8	24.4	6.3
Beef cattle	31.0	32.7	28.9	21.0	8.8	19.3	30.2
Hogs	0.9	1.7	2.5	4.4	9.1	0.2	1.5
Poultry	0.8	1.7	3.3	10.2	6.9	11.0	1.8
Dairy	1.4	7.7	6.0	3.4	9.3	0.7	2.9
General livestock	24.2	11.5	16.4	23.1	28.2	28.0	21.6
Tenure:							

Appendix Table 8. (Continued)

		Debt-to-asset ratio					
Item	No debt	.01 -. 10	.11 -. 40	.41 -. 70	.71 - 1.0	Over 1.0	48-State total
Full owner	72.9	44.8	45.1	57.0	57.4	78.8	64.9
Part owner	21.2	49.8	47.8	28.9	26.0	8.5	28.6
Tenant	5.9	5.5	7.0	14.1	16.5	12.6	6.5
Operator age:							
Less than 35 years	3.9	6.3	6.9	14.1	16.6	19.1	5.2
Full owner	72.9	44.8	45.1	57.0	57.4	78.8	64.9
35 to 44	9.7	12.7	17.7	33.7	29.3	20.5	12.4
45 to 54	21.0	26.2	35.0	26.1	24.7	37.7	23.9
55 to 64 years	31.3	32.2	30.4	21.1	24.3	15.9	30.7
65 years or older	34.1	22.6	10.0	5.0	5.2	6.7	27.8
Mileage to obtain inputs:				*Miles*			
Miles to buy machinery	22.3	26.1	28.0	22.4	35.2	14.6	23.7
Miles to obtain credit	14.2	17.9	17.4	19.8	25.9	17.3	16.0
Miles to farm-related purchasing	16.2	19.4	17.5	16.5	21.0	13.7	16.8

* Total farm financial debt = total farm loan debt + total accounts payable + total accrued interest.

Based on 6,614 observations (6,179 households, 435 non-households). Expansion factor was VER1WT0. Version=1 only. All 48 contiguous States were included in the sample. Rounded percents may not add precisely to 100.

Source: 2007 USDA Agricultural Resource Management Survey.

Appendix Table 9. Farm financial, operator, and structural characteristics for farm operations by number of lenders and loans, 2007

Item		Debt Classification			
	No loans	One lender, one loan	One lender with multiple loans	Multiple lenders and loans	48-State total
			Percent		
Number of farms	1,548,993	399,198	120,148	128,427	2,196,766
Percent of farms	70.5	18.2	5.5	5.8	100.0
Value of production ($ 1,000)	114,312,095	76,912,750	44,791,775	54,197,185	290,213,805
Percent of value of production	39.4	26.5	15.4	18.7	100.0
			Acres per farm		
Land operated per farm	317	500	695	1,035	413
Total farm loan debt	15,370,791	46,986,186	33,680,175	42,537,444	138,574,596
Percent of debt held	11.1	33.9	24.3	30.7	100.0
Farm operation income statement:			*Dollars per farm*		
Gross cash income	72,479	154,750	325,290	394,049	120,056
Less: **Cash expenses**	55,102	128,165	250,187	302,676	93,522
Variable	45,680	102,327	196,703	234,084	75,248
Fixed	9,422	25,838	53,484	68,592	18,274
Equals: **Net cash farm income**	17,377	26,585	75,103	91,373	26,533
Balance sheet characteristics			*$1,000*		
Value of total farm financial assets	1,134,208,467	371,974,302	164,491,753	209,238,797	1,879,913,319
Total farm financial debt*	18,203,612	49,576,858	35,469,958	44,944,736	148,195,164
Accounts payable	2,371,704	1,181,059	779,365	1,131,142	5,463,270

Appendix Table 9. (Continued)

Item		Debt Classification			
	No loans	One lender, one loan	One lender with multiple loans	Multiple lenders and loans	48-State total
Seasonal loans taken and repaid during year	10,085,145	11,410,366	8,175,196	12,039,836	41,710,543
	Percent				
Seasonal loans taken and repaid during year	24.2	27.4	19.6	28.9	100.0
Profitability:					
Return on assets (*percent*)	0.53	1.80	4.50	5.37	1.67
Operating profit margin (*percent*)	4.65	9.49	17.18	19.15	10.41
Debt distributions:					
Sales class:					
$9,999 or less	67.1	45.8	29.2	17.7	58.3
$10,000-$99,999	23.5	30.9	26.9	24.4	25.1
$100,000-$499,999	6.8	15.9	27.2	34.1	11.2
$500,000-$999,999	1.6	4.5	9.3	14.8	3.3
$1,000,000-$4,999,999	0.9	2.5	6.7	8.4	1.9
$5,000,000 or more	0.1	0.3	0.7	0.6	0.2
Farm type:					
Cash grain and soybean	11.0	17.2	27.1	31.0	14.2
Other field crops	24.4	14.8	15.7	11.5	21.5
Item		Debt Classification			

	No loans	One lender, one loan	One lender with multiple loans	Multiple lenders and loans	48-State total
High-value crops	6.5	6.3	6.3	4.9	6.3
Beef cattle	30.7	31.1	28.8	23.0	30.2
Hogs	0.9	2.9	1.3	3.4	1.5
Poultry	0.9	3.8	4.3	3.6	1.8
Dairy	1.5	4.6	7.4	11.2	2.9
General livestock	24.1	19.2	9.0	11.3	21.6
Tenure:					
Full owner	72.4	54.7	38.4	31.4	64.9
Part owner	21.7	36.9	52.9	62.2	28.6
Tenant	5.9	8.4	8.7	6.5	6.5
Operator age:					
Less than 35 years	3.9	8.2	8.3	8.9	5.2
35 to 44	9.7	17.3	23.6	18.8	12.4
45 to 54	21.3	30.6	25.9	32.4	23.9
55 to 64 years	31.6	27.0	32.5	29.9	30.7
65 years or older	33.5	16.9	9.7	10.1	27.8
Mileage to obtain inputs:	*Miles*				
Miles to buy machinery	22.4	25.5	25.8	29.7	23.7
Miles to obtain credit	14.3	18.4	17.1	19.0	16.0
Miles to do farm-related business/purchasing	16.4	17.5	18.0	18.4	16.8

* Total farm financial debt = total farm loan debt + total accounts payable + total accrued interest.

Based on 6,614 observations (6,179 households, 435 non-households). Expansion factor was VER1WT0. Version=1 only. All 48 contiguous States were included in the sample.

Source: 2007 USDA Agricultural Resource Management Survey.

Appendix Table 10. Farm financial, operator, and structural characteristics for farm operations with debt grouped by farm type, 2007

Item	Cash grain and soybean	Other field crops	High value crops	Beef cattle	Hogs	Poultry	Dairy	General livestock	48-State total
Number of farms	149,972	99,700	43,154	195,681	17,941	26,723	43,461	109,716	686,348
Percent of farms	21.9	14.5	6.3	28.5	2.6	3.9	6.3	16.0	100.0
Value of production $ 1,000)	52,410,341	10,886,121	24,134,057	33,718,166	14,430,356	23,211,312	30,598,222	4,756,885	194,145,460
Percent of value of production	27.0	5.6	12.4	17.4	7.4	12.0	15.8	2.5	100.0
		Acres per farm							
Land operated per farm	1,191	497	236	931	323	170	421	186	684
Total farm loan debt	36,747,124	14,282,512	12,603,498	27,210,533	5,860,082	8,828,670	18,372,488	14,669,688	138,574,596
Percen of debt held	26.5	10.3	9.1	19.6	4.2	6.4	13.3	10.6	100.0
Farm operation income statement:		*Dollars per farm*							
Gross cash income	345,114	121,150	566,519	136,582	534,912	220,902	708,787	48,830	242,839
Less: **Cash expenses**	254,889	94,976	451,138	126,252	383,019	152,390	527,070	57,066	192,295
Variable	176,564	70,246	382,612	104,379	320,106	117,662	466,588	38,881	151,309
Fixed	78,325	24,730	68,526	21,874	62,914	34,728	60,482	18,186	40,985
Equals: **Net cash farm income**	90,225	26,174	115,382	10,329	151,893	68,512	181,717	-8,237	50,544

Item	Cash grain and soybean	Other field crops	High value crops	Beef cattle	Hogs	Poultry	Dairy	General livestock	48-State total
Balance sheet characteristics:		*$ 1,000*							
Value of total farm financial assets	240,559,594	87,500,633	67,224,950	208,106,350	24,661,425	29,243,169	91,326,208	65,214,509	813,836,838
Total farm financial debt*	39,491,434	14,987,652	13,401,214	28,483,770	6,179,437	9,141,804	19,177,235	15,283,098	146,145,643
Accounts payable	1,641,884	276,657	419,610	456,901	143,551	48,272	253,567	173,306	3,413,749
Seasonal loans taken and repaid during year	13,990,608	3,239,670	3,009,221	6,829,433	1,123,574	498,702	2,436,395	926,910	32,054,512
		Percent							
Seasonal loans taken and repaid during year	43.6	10.1	9.4	21.3	3.5	1.6	7.6	2.9	100.0
Profitability:					*Percent*				
Return on assets	6.53	2.15	5.93	0.09	10.46	4.40	4.58	-1.51	3.49
Operating profit margin	24.95	13.50	15.60	0.63	24.68	19.35	12.95	[a]13.67	15.05
Debt distributions:									
Sales class:									
$9,999 or less	4.8	59.3	17.1	38.0	35.4	17.1	0.0	84.6	36.7
$10,000-$99,999	27.4	26.9	41.5	45.5	12.6	2.1	19.6	10.1	28.8
$100,000-$499,999	46.3	7.2	22.3	11.8	15.2	29.2	57.6	3.7	21.7
$500,000-$999,999	16.2	4.1	9.7	2.8	13.8	29.1	10.4	0.5	7.8

Appendix Table 10. (Continued)

Item	Cash grain and soybean	Other field crops	High value crops	Beef cattle	Hogs	Poultry	Dairy	General livestock	48-State total
$1,000,000-$4,999,999	5.1	2.5	7.6	1.4	21.2	21.4	10.3	1.1	4.6
$5,000,000 or more	0.1	0.0	1.7	0.5	1.8	1.1	2.0	0.1	0.5
Tenure:									
Full owner	19.2	62.3	63.3	43.9	47.9	76.1	15.9	78.4	47.5
Part owner	66.5	34.1	27.4	48.0	42.5	23.3	73.1	19.9	44.7
Tenant	14.3	3.7	9.3	8.0	9.5	0.6	11.0	1.7	7.8
Operator age:									
Less than 35 years	11.5	6.2	2.1	8.1	2.3	9.6	11.7	7.0	8.1
35 to 44	17.7	14.8	11.0	14.6	26.7	38.2	18.9	25.5	18.3
45 to 54	29.2	29.3	36.8	26.9	45.5	24.4	38.8	30.8	30.2
55 to 64 years	26.6	35.5	33.7	33.2	17.5	21.7	21.1	26.6	29.4
65 years or older	15.1	14.4	16.4	17.2	8.0	6.0	9.5	10.1	13.9
Mileage to obtain inputs:		*Miles*							
Miles to buy machinery	27.6	21.5	28.9	28.5	29.6	21.1	27.3	25.3	26.5
Miles to obtain credit	16.9	14.8	19.7	20.5	14.5	18.8	19.7	17.6	18.1
Miles to do farm-related business/purchasing	13.9	15.1	30.8	21.1	15.9	15.6	22.9	15.6	18.1

* Total farm financial debt = total farm loan debt + total accounts payable + total accrued interest.

Based on 3,570 observations (3,363 households, 207 non-households). Expansion factor was VER1WT0. Version=1 only. Source: 2007 USDA Agricultural Resource Management Survey.

Appendix Table 11. Increased concentration of U.S. farm debt, by year, 1998–2007

Item	1998	1999	2000	2001	2002	2003	2004	2005	2006	2007
Number of farms	2,054,711	2,186,951	2,166,061	2,149,388	2,152,415	2,120,819	2,107,925	2,094,876	2,082,674	2,196,766
Number of farms with debt	911,291	925,139	919,979	897,250	928,304	871,408	832,095	780,806	732,740	666,898
Percent of farms with debt	44	42	42	42	43	41	39	37	35	30
	Dollars per farm									
Farm financial debt	55,541	51,374	57,031	58,610	65,314	65,091	65,684	64,657	69,961	67,348
Farm financial assets	520,470	497,330	535,807	559,421	547,726	628,840	708,363	777,669	878,119	845,024
Net worth (equity)	464,930	445,956	478,776	500,811	482,412	563,749	642,678	713,012	808,158	777,676
Net cash farm income	16,480	14,193	13,550	16,133	12,086	16,262	24,529	24,439	19,090	27,594
Value of commodities produced	90,960	80,605	81,847	89,974	84,770	88,006	107,071	102,772	108,536	132,900
	$ million									
Farm financial debt	114,120	112,352	123,532	125,976	140,583	138,047	138,458	135,448	145,706	147,949
Farm financial assets	1,069,416	1,087,637	1,160,590	1,202,414	1,178,933	1,333,656	1,493,175	1,629,119	1,828,836	1,856,340
Net worth (equity)	955,296	975,285	1,037,058	1,076,437	1,038,351	1,195,609	1,354,718	1,493,671	1,683,131	1,708,391
Net cash farm income	33,861	31,040	29,349	34,676	26,014	34,488	51,706	51,196	39,759	60,619
Value of commodities produced	186,897	176,280	177,286	193,390	182,461	186,644	225,698	215,295	226,045	291,954
	Ratio									
Debt/asset ratio	0.107	0.103	0.106	0.105	0.119	0.104	0.093	0.083	0.080	0.080
Debt/equity ratio	0.119	0.115	0.119	0.117	0.135	0.115	0.102	0.091	0.087	0.087

Appendix Table 11. (Continued)

Item	1998	1999	2000	2001	2002	2003	2004	2005	2006	2007
Debt/value of commodities ratio	0.611	0.637	0.697	0.651	0.770	0.740	0.613	0.629	0.645	0.507
All farms Number of farms	2,054,711	2,186,951	2,166,061	2,149,388	2,152,415	2,120,819	2,107,925	2,094,876	2,082,674	2,196,791
Gini coefficient	0.848	0.850	0.858	0.853	0.854	0.859	0.865	0.876	0.879	0.901
Only farms with debt:										
Number of farms with debt	911,291	925,139	919,979	897,250	928,304	871,408	832,095	780,806	732,740	666,898
Gini coefficient of farms with debt	0.657	0.646	0.665	0.648	0.661	0.656	0.658	0.668	0.657	0.674
	Percent									
Farms by income solvency class:										
Favorable	59	62	60	62	59	62	66	65	62	61
Marginal income	33	31	32	29	31	29	28	28	32	34
Marginal solvency	4	4	3	3	5	4	3	3	3	2
Vulnerable	5	4	5	5	5	5	3	4	3	3
Sample size	11,812	10,251	10,309	7,699	12,391	18,459	20,579	22,843	21,734	18,709

All 48 contiguous States were included in the sample. Alaska, Hawaii, and U.S. territories are excluded from the surveys. Rounded percents may not add precisely to 100.

Source: 1998–2007 USDA Farm Costs and Returns Survey/Agricultural Resource Management Survey.

End Notes

[1] For more information on calculating the sector-level farm financial statement, see the documentation at www. ers. usda. gov/Briefing/FarmIncome/ Glossary/def_bsht. htm or ERS Publication Number 671, Volume 11 of Major Statistical Series of the U.S. Department of Agriculture.

[2] For more information on the ARMS, please visit the ARMS Briefing Room at www. ers. usda. gov/Briefing/ ARMS/

[3] An updated forecast of 2009 farm sector debt will be available on November 24, 2009.

[4] The ARMS and its predecessor survey, the Farm Costs and Returns Survey, were developed to provide data needed to derive a farm-level balance sheet consistent with a farm's income statement. Data obtained from respondents to USDA survey instruments provide a basis for assessing the level and distribution of debt among farms and in relation to income, returns to assets, and debt service.

[5] ARMS based, farm-level estimates of debt and associated farm and farm-household finance data for 2008 will be released publicly through the ERS website on November 24, 2009

[6] See www. ers. usda. gov/Briefing/ FarmIncome/Wealth. htm for a discussion of specific sources of data for farm business assets and debt.

[7] This is the nominal amount of net income that accrues to farms as business establishments. It does not include any portion of net cash income generated from agricultural activities that accrue to other stakeholders in U.S. agriculture, such as the income earned by contractors that establish production contracts with farmers. ERS has estimated that contractors received 11. 9 percent of the net value added generated by U.S. agriculture in 2007.

[8] There is more information on the DRCU in the Farm Income and Costs Briefing Room, www. ers. usda. gov/ Briefing/FarmIncome/Wealth. htm

[9] An outgrowth of the 1980s farm financial crisis was to enact programs enabling lenders to obtain a guarantee against the loss of a predominant share of principal and interest on a loan. In these programs, a farmer or rancher applies to a lender for debt financing for either farm ownership or farm operating purposes. The lender arranges the guarantee. Businesses are eligible to obtain a guarantee if they have an acceptable audit history, as determined by the lender, and are otherwise unable to obtain a loan without a guarantee. The availability of guarantees for lenders making loans to farmers that may otherwise be credit-constrained not only helps expand farm loan volume but also lessens the risk of loan losses for participating lenders.

[11] Debt-asset ratios up to 70 percent may be acceptable in some farming circumstances where income and cash flows are more readily available to meet debt service requirements; although lenders become more cautious with debt-asset ratios over 50 percent (Blocker, et al., 2003).

End Notes for Appendix

[1] Field work to enumerate ARMS questionnaires is conducted during February-April. Content of the ARMS is developed to inquire about the prior calendar year, with asset and debt outstanding questions having a reference date of December 31.

[2] Respondents would choose any of four reasons, including more than one reason if applicable: having sufficient funds without loans, could not obtain new or additional credit, high transaction costs, or risk associated with debt

[3] AELOS is a special survey conducted by USDA's NASS that interviews owners of farmland, and includes both owner-operators and nonoperator landlords.

INDEX

D

E

F

G

H

I

L

M

N

O

P

Q

R

S

T

U

V

W